Golden Children

Legacy of Ethnic Studies, SF State

Juanita Tamayo Lott

Eastwind Books of Berkeley
Berkeley, California

Golden Children: Legacy of Ethnic Studies, SF State
by Juanita Tamayo Lott

For more information or to book an author event,
contact www.AsiaBookCenter.com

Front cover photo: "SF State College Fists" taken on "Bloody Tuesday,"
December 3, 1968. Photo by Nacio Jan Brown

Back cover photo: TWLF veterans from SF State and UC Berkeley
at Asian Law Caucus, July 25, 2018, S.F. Photo by Harvey Dong

ISBN: 9780996351782 (paperback)

10 9 8 7 6 5 4 3 2 1

DEDICATION

Dedicated to the parents, children, and grandchildren of the students, faculty, and staff who went on strike at San Francisco State November 6, 1968 – March 20, 1969. The strikers demanded equal access to public higher education, more senior faculty of color, and a new curriculum that embraced the history and cultures of all Americans, including US racial/ethnic minorities.

ACKNOWLEDGMENTS

San Francisco State strikers, alumni and/or current students, faculty and staff:

With special thanks to Malcolm Collier, Meredith Eliassen, Kenneth Monteiro, Alex Sanchez, and SF State DIVA Archives; Rosalie Alfonso, Roger Alvarado, Teresa Carillo, Miguel Casuso, Jeff Chan, Alex Cherian, Laureen Chew, Gordon Chin, Phil Chin, Curtis Choy, Irene Dea Collier, Robert Keith Collins, Terry Collins, Robert Corrigan, Jerry Dear, Lorraine Dong, Jason Ferreira, Dawn-Elissa Fischer, Jimmy Garrett, Nancy Gerber, Daniel P. Gonzales, Juan Gonzales, Danny Glover, Christine Harris, James Hirabayashi, Lane Hirabayashi, Robert Ilumin, Judy Juanita, Mark Kelleher, Genny Lim, Ellie Luis, Daryl Maeda, Sharon Gold Martinas, Katynka Martinez, Bette Inouye Matsuoka, Dick Miner, Nancy Mirabal, Steve Nakajo, Penny Nakatsu, Catherine Powell, Ronald Quidachay, Belinda Reyes, Dorothy Ross, Don Scoble, Benny Stewart, Amy Sueyoshi, Ramona Tascoe, Terrence Terauchi, Ray Thompson, Arnold Townsend, Dorothy Tsuruta, Jerry Varnado, Richard Wada, Helene Whitson, Alfred Wong, Mason Wong, George Woo, Gerry Wright and Grace Jeanmee Yoo.

Others:

Walter Allen, Judy Blanchard, Nacio Jan Brown, Cathy Ceniza Choy, Belva Davis, Frank Dawson, Bea Dong, Harvey Dong, Abby Ginzberg, Betty Lee Hawks, Barbara Jue, Judi Mozesson, Canta Pian, Rob Santos, Shizue Siegel, Michael O'Donnell Smith, C. Matthew Snipp, Bob Wax, Lisa White, Ellen Dionne Wu, Henry Wu and Judy Yung.

Non-San Francisco State University Librarians/Archivists/ Researchers:

Chris Doan, archivist, Archives of the Archdiocese of San Francisco; Latasha Hill, researcher and the staff of the US Census Bureau; Sine Hwang Jensen, librarian, Ethnic Studies Library, UC Berkeley; and Christina Moretta, photo curator, Susan Goldstein, city archivist and the staff of the History Center, San Francisco Public Library

AUTHOR BIOGRAPHY

Juanita Tamayo Lott is a retired senior federal demographer/statistician. Her works from poetry to statistical analysis are in anthologies and professional journals since the 1970s. She is the author *of Asian Americans: From Racial Category to Multiple Identities,* 1998; *Common Destiny: Filipino American Generations,* 2006; and *Filipinos in Washington, DC* with Rita Cacas, 2009. The Juanita Tamayo Lott Collection resides in the Asian American and Pacific Islander Collection, Asian Division, The Library of Congress, Washington, DC.

GOLDEN CHILDREN

CONTENTS

GOLDEN CHILDREN

INTRODUCTION

On May 4 and 15, 2016, San Francisco State University (SF State) and the world-famous San Francisco Castro Theater screened the award-winning documentary, *Agents of Change*. This film tells the timely and inspiring story of how successful civic protest for self-determination and representation in the form of a strike led to establishing the first School of Ethnic Studies at SF State (1968) and the Afro American Studies Center at Cornell University (1969). After the screenings, several folks, including San Francisco poet Genny Lim, asked me about the participation and contributions of Asian Americans, Latinos, Native peoples, and women in the strike for ethnic studies at SF State in 1968–1969. During this time in spring 2016, students of ethnic studies at SF State were just completing another strike, including a hunger strike, to protest cutbacks to faculty and resources to the College of Ethnic Studies. This time, minorities and women were visible leaders. They called themselves Third World Liberation Front (TWLF) 2016, honoring their connection to the TWLF 1968–1969 SF State student-led strike.

Much of what is known publicly about minority student activism in higher education in the late 1960s and early 1970s is mainly attributed to Black male students and White allies fighting against a White establishment. Erroneously, the general public has long thought the struggles began at UC Berkeley and other elite institutions of higher education. Much of the public documentation of this period during and immediately after the strike was limited primarily to the mainstream media, White college administrators, and the National Commission on the Causes and Prevention of Violence. As succinctly stated by Emeritus Professor Carlos Muñoz, Jr., Department of Ethnic Studies, UC Berkeley, much of the coverage of minority student activism was secular coverage of law and order in the First World. One notable exception was *An End to Silence: The San Francisco State Student Movement in the 60s*, authored by then SF State students, William Barlow and Peter Shapiro. As respective associate editor and editor of a 1968–1969 SF State student newspaper, *Open Process*, they were deeply and personally involved. Their book "places the strike in the context of the growth of the student movement at San

Francisco State since 1960 and the concomitant development of the crisis in California's public education system which in fact made the strike necessary." A more recent exception is *Activist State (Documentary: 1968 San Francisco State Student Strike)* by student Jonathan Craig, produced with fellow students and faculty advisors, namely Grace Provenzano, in 2009 in the Broadcast and Electronic Communications Arts Department, SF State. This brief documentary includes interviews by TWLF strike leaders from their perspective in the 21st century. Another student documentary, *On Strike! The Birth of Ethnic Studies,* directed by Cristian Alvarado with fellow students and faculty advisor Nancy Mirabal, provides various perspectives. As striker Gordon Chin noted in his 2015 book, *Building Community, Chinatown Style,* "With all due respect to UC Berkeley's Free Speech Movement, which came earlier in 1964, the San Francisco State Student Strike was different. It was led by students of color with support from the Students for a Democratic Society and other white progressive student groups. This was the awakening of the Black, La Raza, Asian, and Native American students, a coalition of emerging movements and people."

Written as a memoir, the purpose of this book is to remember and to pay tribute to the thousands of unsung youth, men and women—working class and middle class students, faculty, staff, and their supporters and their far-reaching legacy at an internationally-known public state university. They were willing to stand up; be arrested; be imprisoned; lose financial aid; lose their jobs; and, in the case of BSU/TWLF leader Jack Alexis, be deported. SF State has long been a leader for social justice and active civic engagement. Most of these unsung heroes and heroines have never been officially or publicly recognized. Many of them have passed on. It was only after forty years, in October 2009, that the student and faculty leaders and foot soldiers of the strike were formally acknowledged at a gala reception at the St. Francis Yacht Club. Founding Dean James A. Hirabayashi was honored while the Black Student Union/Third World Liberation Front leaders were formally recognized and thanked. That event, along with the release of *Agents of Change* in 2016, the SF State TWLF 2016 student strike, and the February 11, 2018 farewell and appreciation reception for College of Ethnic

Studies Dean Kenneth Monteiro, was the impetus to share personal and collective memories and experiences. My insider, subjective synthesis is complemented by external and public information.

Thanks to prescient and passionate archivists and historians, rich data on this period have been captured. These include the SF State Library Strike Archives and Labor Archives Collections and the DIVA (Digital Image and Video Archive) Collection of the Academic Technology at SF State, publications of Asian American Studies and the College of Ethnic Studies, SF State, as well as interviews conducted by faculty and staff of the College of Ethnic Studies. The San Francisco Public Library History Center archives provide complementary documentation and ephemera.

According to the DIVA introduction to the SF State College Strike Collection, "During 1968–1969, San Francisco State College was a focus for national attention as the campus erupted in turmoil. Initially students threatened to strike to stop the College's cooperation with the draft but discontent broadened to embrace the concerns of minority students and the eventual strike is often referred to as 'the Third World strike.'" It may be tempting to see this period romantically, as just another example of students around the world engaged in the anti-Vietnam War movement, revolutions in Third World colonies, the American Civil Rights Movement, and the counter culture movement.

In fact, the SF State student-led strike and the reasons for the strike and its demands were not romantic but sobering. It occurred while the United States was waging war across the Pacific, adamantly sending its youth to an undeclared war. While finite, the strike's impact was not fleeting. It is embodied in the College of Ethnic Studies and every student, staff, faculty or community member associated with the college in negotiations over the strike demands—to implement the principles for self-determination and relevant education by manifesting a 'School of Third World Studies.' In the last fifty years, the students, staff, and faculty of ethnic studies at SF State have withstood countless challenges with limited resources and declining budgets.

The first challenge was not having all of the fifteen strike demands of the Black Students Union (BSU) and the Third World Liberation Front (TWLF) met. The second was that the "School of Third World

Studies" was watered down to the "School of Ethnic Studies." Despite these obstacles and amid great sacrifice and struggle personally and institutionally, the relevance of the strike continues today. Moreover, the College of Ethnic Studies has not only survived but thrived and expanded. Subsequently, as the ethnic studies discipline became established in higher education, younger scholars began to contribute to the scholarship of this phenomenon that was borne from a successful student-led strike supported by a variety of community members.

The struggles, challenges, successes, and legacy of these pioneers continue today as we celebrate fifty years of the College of Ethnics Studies at SF State. Uniquely and regrettably, this is the only College of Ethnic Studies in the world. Scholars, researchers, and practitioners come from all over the globe to learn how this college came to be; how it continues to thrive; and how it remains relevant to the future of not just higher education but to an informed democratic citizenry, a nation of service, and the competitive human capital of the United States of America.

Drawing on Third World, especially Asian American, experiences, I first describe the context and environment that nurtured these students and their communities. Second, I argue that the call to action to establish and sustain an enduring Ethnic Studies/Third World Studies at SF State was not primarily ideological but practical because of its grass roots origins and its thousands of unsung heroes and heroines. Certainly the nuts and bolts for creating the College of Ethnic Studies were provided by adults and youngsters from their respective geographic and racial/ethnic communities in the Bay Area, who brought their experiences of resistance and community organizing. Third, I highlight the often-overlooked reality that it is the younger generation who makes changes. The children often lead us, as was the case in 1968–1969, 2016, and the years in between and after. This crucial point takes into account the non-academic, infrastructure legacy of the then School and later College of Ethnic Studies in the lives of everyday people, not just the academic community. Fourth, I focus on students of color who, strengthened by the self-affirmation and political education that came from being scholars in ethnic studies, heeded the call to work in the larger community, including

California and Washington, DC.

Finally, I provide examples over four decades to depict the wide-reaching legacy of ethnic studies at SF State. Such an impact becomes real and poignant to us in specific moments of legacy and remembrance.

One example was on April 23, 2017, when over five hundred family, friends and colleagues attended the memorial service for Philip P. Choy, who, with Him Mark Lai, taught the first course on the history of the Chinese in America at San Francisco State in fall 1969. Students from his first and last classes, and those in between, testified to the importance of learning this history and how this knowledge and Philip's inspirational teaching style motivated them in their personal lives and subsequent careers and community work.

Despite the Southeast Asian war, from the perspective of half a century later, 1968–1969 was a more innocent period before social media and narrower concerns of celebrity status, careers, self-actualization, and the bottom line. It was a period where golden children were the first to go to college in their families; were more humble and appreciative of our parents' sacrifices to send us to college despite long standing institutional racism; and were more sensitive to the larger needs of our lower income and middle class communities. We believed in making love not war. We believed we would transform and prevail. As we celebrate the golden anniversaries of the TWLF Strike and College of Ethnic Studies at SF State, its golden children—students, faculty, staff, and communities—were and continue to be not just Agents of Change but also Agents of Continuity.

GOLDEN CHILDREN

CHAPTER 1

Being In The Right Place At The Right Time

Manuel and the Hulk

On January 23, 1969 Manuel Difuntorum and I were part of the students, faculty, and staff of San Francisco State College with outside supporters and observers, quietly and peacefully gathered on the grassy campus quad. Almost simultaneously, everything tightened and loosened. A peaceful, nonviolent demonstration in front of the Speaker's Platform at the quad in the center of campus was interrupted by the San Francisco Police Department Tactical Squad. Students, other demonstrators, and interested bystanders were surrounded. Manuel quickly grabbed me and we ran away from the quad to Holloway Avenue where his car, nicknamed "The Hulk," was parked. According to Bob Ilumin, a member of the Third World Liberation Front Central Committee, representing the Philippine American Collegiate Endeavor (PACE), "While you guys drove away I was caught up surrounded by S.F. Police including those on horseback. I happen to be one of the speakers that day. About two hundred (sic) were arrested and were bused to the Hall of Justice (Bryant Street). I ended spend (sic) the weekend at the County Jail. The time was one of great opportunity which raised the social consciousness of the Nation. The unique thing was it brought together people of color joining together and delivering a strong message of disenfranchisement and limited opportunities in the Nation."[1] The Hulk was a dark, faded, blue/green big American car, two door, bench seat, and noisy. Manuel pulled me into the passenger side. Making a U-turn, he quickly drove off across 19th Avenue amid the clanging of the M-Oceanview street car and the chants of "On Strike! Shut It Down!" and "The Pigs Are on Campus!"

That day was captured in media around the world. We lucked out. We didn't get arrested like Bob and over four hundred students

---

1   Robert Illumin, personal communication with author, August 7, 2017.

and community members. Instead, Manuel and I went to Central City. In addition to being full time students, we were members of Pilipino American Collegiate Endeavor (PACE), one of the student organizations of the Third World Liberation Front. PACE representatives served on the Third World Liberation Front Central Committee, the umbrella student organization that led the strike on November 6, 1968 and negotiated the strike settlement with the SF State administration on March 20, 1969. The other student organizations comprising the TWLF Central Committee were the Black Student Union (BSU), the Intercollegiate Chinese for Social Action (ICSA), the Asian American Political Alliance (AAPA), Latin American Student Organization (LASO), the Mexican American Student Confederation (MASC) and the Native American Student Organization (NASO).

Manuel drove across Junipero Serra Boulevard downhill on to Portola Drive then to Market Street and angled south towards the Mission. That day, Manuel and I were fulfilling the strike principles of self-determination and relevant education by going to Central City. Central City is now known as South of Market, SOMA. In 1969, Central City was outside the center. It was home to industrial San Francisco composed of many side streets—alleys really—with female names including famous ladies of the night such as Minna and other San Franciscans such as Clementina. Interspersed but not highly visible among the commercial establishments were residences for all manner of people and families, not just single room occupancies primarily for single males. Between industrial buildings and garages, two and three-story flats were squeezed in for Samoan and Filipino working class families, many of which had served or were currently serving in the military.

Manuel and I headed for St. Patrick's Youth Center on Clementina Street. Young men on the street recognized The Hulk. We were met by the youth director, Don Heard, a middle-aged Black man who made sure this oasis for young people to congregate was opened. He welcomed us to meet with some of the mainly Filipino teenage boys playing basketball. Manuel had applications for admission to SF State. After greeting them in Tagalog and Ilocano, he delivered an impassioned talk on the importance of college education as an alternative to an otherwise predictable future

2

of inner city, lower income status youth. The Vietnam War was waging and many boys and young men of color with limited horizons saw the military as an option out of San Francisco neighborhoods like Central City, the Mission, the Fillmore, Hunter's Point and Chinatown. The other option was going to "Juvie," as the San Francisco Youth Guidance Center was locally known. The students in PACE and the other Third World Liberation Front organizations were actively showing their younger brothers and sisters how to expand their horizons for self-determination by including the possibility of a college education. Their actions on campus were not limited to accessing seats for non-traditional students and positions for non-traditional faculty in the public, tax-supported institutions of higher education in California. Integral to the strike and ethnic studies at San Francisco State was to connect the college back to serving the needs of Third World communities and other populations under-represented in higher education so they could become engaged residents and citizens. At its core, San Francisco State was an institution of higher education created to serve the needs of the larger community. For students of color, SF State offered a way to serve the needs of their disenfranchised communities.

This was accomplished in part through tutoring programs of elementary and secondary students by college students and by engaging their parents and elders to speak up for needed social services in areas like Chinatown and the Mission. Tutoring programs were not an innovative idea of BSU/TWLF but of the Experimental College, where initially, mainly white students tutored students of color. The innovation was the fact that it was BSU/TWLF students returning to their neighborhoods to address community needs. It provided the children with young adults of color who looked like them and shared their life experiences. They were insiders, not outsiders, do-gooders, colonizers or missionaries. They were leaders and role models. This innovation represented self-sufficiency and self-determination, and to some, revolution.

At St. Patrick's Youth Center, the young men listened respectfully but shyly. Some had never thought of college as an option. Their objective was to just finish high school and get a job to assist their parents to support their often large and immigrant families. A few took the applications. Manuel said we would be happy to answer any questions and help fill out the forms. I don't know how many actually filled out and submitted their forms. This was not an uncommon experience of other students of the TWLF/BSU trying to help youngsters by presenting the messages to stay in school; get off the streets; stay out of prison; and think of college. Despite a feeling of uncertainty and maybe even failure about being able to connect with these youth, SF State had enrolled 128 special admissions, mainly minority, students under the Educational Opportunity Program by the spring 1969 semester due to outreach of students to their minority communities. In addition, San Francisco State formally supported the creation of a School of Ethnic Studies that began operation in the fall semester, 1969.

Historical Context

There are many perspectives on who won and who lost the student-led strike at San Francisco State and what was won and what was lost. There will continue to be so as the founding generations pass on and new generations of students and faculty with different perspectives and life experiences interpret this historical event. The reality is that the strike and the establishment of the then School of Ethnic Studies (later the College of Ethnic Studies) came at the right place at the right time. They had powerful precedents.

One was World War II. For the most part, the students at San Francisco State in 1968 were born during or after World War II, when the United States became a major world power. Patriotism and citizenship were extolled. The military was de-segregated during the war to include soldiers of color, even if they were confined to their own regiments. Soldiers of color were part of the liberation forces of Europe and Asia. They had seen the larger world. They had been welcomed as liberators on other continents. Soldiers of color fought against Nazism and Fascism. For Asians born outside of the US, military service was their ticket to citizenship, thwarting the historic label of "aliens ineligible for citizenship." At a time when all men were eligible for the draft, the idea of defending the United States and supporting its soldiers was uppermost in the minds of most residents of the United States and became a way to unify the nation. On the other hand, World War II brought the chilling and divisive Executive Order 9066, a presidential executive order effectively removing 120,000 Japanese Americans from their West Coast homes and placing them in internment camps as resident enemy aliens. This historical experience played directly into the demands for and importance of Japanese American/Asian American Studies at San Francisco State. This period of history had not been recognized or taught as a watershed civics lesson.

At the same time, on the home front, the nation was united by the creation of jobs to satisfy a market for war production. For example, the Rosie the Riveter World War II Home Front National Historical Park in Richmond, CA today depicts how women and people of color in the Bay Area supported fighting troops by their labor in the Kaiser Shipyards. Migrating from the South and across the nation, the workers in four shipyards in Richmond produced 747 ships for carrying general cargo and military munitions, more than any other complex in the United States. It allowed people excluded from traditionally white male occupations to gain skills and entry into the working and middle classes.

On a more sober note, across the Pacific, with the dropping of atomic bombs on the Japanese cities of Hiroshima and Nagasaki, the idea of limited war forever had been replaced by ultimate war. Civil defense drills were common in the 1950s with Americans trained to listen to emergency alarms and head for fallout shelters in case of a massive nuclear attack. It was estimated that over 12 million Americans would die in such an attack.[2] For children born after the atom bomb, life was precarious. Would they be like their fathers, whose response to the destruction and deaths of another world war was to come home and live life fully, bringing forth the many children of the Baby Boomer generation, and creating the economic expansion? Or would they respond otherwise?

Caution was the order of the day in the post-World War II era of the Cold War. Given the House Un-American Activities Committee (HUAC)

---

2 History.com Editors, "First nationwide civil defense drill held." *HISTORY*, Nov 13, 2009. https://www.history.com/this-day-in-history/first-nationwide-civil-defense-drill-held.

created in 1938 to investigate alleged disloyalty and subversive activities on the part of private citizens, public employees, and organizations suspected of having Communist ties, it was no surprise that the Cold War focused on "Who was a Communist? Who was an American?" and specifically, "Who was a Loyal American?" Under the aggressive accusations by then Senator Joseph McCarthy (1947–1957), Americans again had their allegiance and citizenship questioned. For people of color this meant again defending their role and right as Americans. The Cold War coincided with the post-World War II revolutions of Third World colonies in Africa, Asia, and Latin America against European and North American colonizers. This revolutionary history was embraced by peoples of color in the United States and other nations, reaffirming the existence of alternate worldviews to the Eurocentric, White Anglo Saxon Protestant (WASP) worldview.

A second precedent that supported the San Francisco State strike happening at the right place and the right time were initiatives related to peace and prosperity. Post World War II, the United States became an economic power as other nations focused on recovering from the human toll and infrastructure devastation of war. Through policies such as the Marshall Plan for Western European nations (officially the European Recovery Program) and much smaller grants and credits to Asian countries, the US displayed its growing economic and political power. It also suggested confidence in making a difference at home and abroad.

In his 1961 presidential inaugural address, President John Fitzgerald Kennedy challenged the children of World War II veterans and others by boldly stating, "My fellow Americans, ask not what your country can do for you, ask what you can do for your country." The young president laid out a vision of a New Frontier where Americans were world citizens via serving in the Peace Corps and pioneers exploring the moon and outer space via NASA. White and minority college students heeded the call to join the Peace Corps. United States Air Force Captain Edward Joseph Dwight, Jr was selected as the first African American to be trained as an American astronaut in 1961.

A major international initiative fueled by and also eventually contributing to the prosperity of the United States was passage of the Immigration and Naturalization Act of 1965, which abolished the quota system based on national origins established by the American Immigration Policy of 1924. The earlier policy restricted immigration of Southern and Eastern Europeans and Africans and specifically excluded Asians. The consequence of the 1965 act was a flow of new Americans, a new labor force—people of color with multi-lingual, multi-cultural, and interdisciplinary skills. They were critical human capital to power the post-war economic prosperity. They were essential for a post-industrial yet still labor-intensive economy. They were a significant factor in the future ability of the US to compete in a global economy, as ongoing immigration provided not just needed person power but technological and other innovations.

At the domestic level, with Head Start, the Kennedy administration promoted comprehensive early childhood education, health, nutrition and parental involvement to low-income children and their families. In the post-war era, a child-oriented American society emerged. Its most cherished possession was its children. As the future generation, America's children were the nation's human capital and best investment for a prosperous economy. Upon Kennedy's assassination, President Lyndon Johnson embarked on the Great Society and the War on Poverty with major reforms aligned with achieving a healthy, competitive workforce and economy including the passage of Civil Rights legislation in public accommodations, employment, education, and housing, and the passage of Medicare. President Johnson expanded upon President Franklin Roosevelt's safety net with Social Security as its hallmark. This was an America who could do great things with and for all of its people. Unfortunately, this expectation was overblown, as the riches of America got caught up in a protracted war in Southeast Asia. American leaders lied to their citizens about intervening in the Vietnamese civil war, resulting in a tremendous loss of lives on all sides and the loss of trust by the American people in their government for decades.

Nonetheless, victory and productivity in World War II, growing up in a prosperous, post-war United States, along with political organizing skills built during the Civil Rights and anti-Vietnam War movements, provided excellent reference points for the "Can Do" attitude of the strikers and founders of ethnic studies at San Francisco State. This was a United States where my dad (and other dads of color like him)—a citizen, military veteran, and union employee—could buy a house in San Francisco and have his children graduate from public college. It was a time when California believed that public higher education should be free for its youth and that its children were its greatest human capital and long-term investment. An equal but less-recognized precedent to this unique historical context was the cultural context.

The Cultural Context

In my talks over the years with fellow strikers and other activists of color, what has evolved is the effect of the larger cultural context. As children of the atom bomb, we found comfort in the culture of imaginary heroes and super heroes first in comics and then on screen. These personalities infiltrated our childhood and young adulthood, not only with the Halloween costumes we wore to emulate our heroes but also with the values of justice they represented. While we had Captain America, there was also Superman—an undocumented alien from another planet. There was Wonder Woman, a princess, an Amazon, and the half-alien daughter of Ares, the god of war. Despite these non-traditional characteristics, Wonder Woman was a bona fide member of the Justice League of America. We were also intrigued and inspired by fully human, non-super heroes such as Batman, Robin, the Phantom, and the Lone Ranger, in part because they were masked. We could have been them, even beyond our Halloween capes and costumes. With comics, so much was left to our childhood imaginations. We created our own faces, our own images of super heroes and everyday heroes fighting for truth, justice, and the American way. We were allowed to be masked and unmasked.

Comic book super heroes still resonate for today's young people of color. For example, Ryan Coogler, the young award-winning director of *Fruitvale Station*, *Creed* and *Black Panther*, who grew up in Oakland, CA, noted at the 2017 Comic-Con in San Diego that part of his youth was spent in search of black superheroes at a comic book store near his East Bay elementary school called Dr. Comics & Mr. Games. He discovered the Black Panther, T'Challa, the first black superhero in mainstream

American comics. Created by writer-editor Stan Lee and artist and co-plotter Jack Kirby, the Black Panther first appeared in Marvel Comics' Fantastic Four #52 (July 1966).

Just as social media today is a major means of obtaining information and communication for the Millennial Generation, radio and television were the purview of Baby Boomers. They were identified as the new target consumer audience known as "teenagers." Television was not just the newest consumer technology and status symbol. It was also the baby sitter for many children of working class parents who had to hold more than one job or work non-traditional hours to support their families. Being in California—the home of Hollywood—we saw a lot of children's shows. Similar to identifying with comic book characters, we looked at the World of Disney's Mickey Mouse Club and fantasized that amid the blonde and blue-eyed Mouseketeers, perhaps dark-haired, dark-eyed Annette Funicello might be a Latina, or even Filipina. We watched westerns—cowboy programs like the *Cisco Kid and Pancho* with their Spanish-named horses Diablo and Loco. Weekly we tuned in to *Elfego Baca*, *Broken Arrow* with Indian agent Tom Jeffords and Chiricahua Apache chief Cochise, the *Lone Ranger and Tonto*, and *Zorro*. We cheered and connected, even if Michael Ansara was Syrian (Cochise) and Guy Williams (Zorro) was Italian American. While the actual Elfego Baca was a Latino from New Mexico, Robert Loggia was an Italian American.

Among the non-cowboy programs, we cheered, laughed, and danced along with multi-talented Cuban bandleader and musician Desi Arnaz in *I Love Lucy*. As adolescents we had to go to the future and other worlds to see ourselves in Star Trek's George Takei's Hikaru Sulu and Nichelle Nichols' Uhura. We came down to earth with *I Spy* co-stars Robert Culp and Bill Cosby. As young adults going to the cinema, we absorbed *In the Heat of the Night* with Sidney Poitier and Rod Steiger.

Television brought the war in Vietnam to our living rooms, depicting the many faces of the color of war. It also bore witness to government violence against Americans at home. Television-documented milestones of the Civil Rights Movement included Bull Connor of Birmingham, AL ordering water hoses and attack dogs on hundreds of peaceful student protestors in 1963. It captured the 1964 and 1968 urban riots in inner cities and the police brutality during the 1968 Democratic Convention in Chicago. Film footage showed Chicago Mayor Richard Daley sending out police to beat unarmed peaceful protestors singing, "Blowing in the Wind." Such volatile, dangerous news paved the way for sending Black and other people of color to be reporters in print and screen. And then these reporters moved on to be anchors, first on local television and then the national networks. As Jim Vance, long-time, award-winning anchor at Washington, DC's WRC-TB (Channel 4) succinctly noted, "We had burned Watts, Detroit and Newark. They were looking for a black face."[3]

Along with the larger cultural context, the Golden Children of the Golden State were molded by the local cultural context. It was a nurturing and inspiring context of Gold Mountain, painstakingly chronicled by early Chinese American author, Betty Lee Sung, and the Golden Gate Bridge lovingly described by California State Librarian/Historian Kevin Starr.

In brief, the local cultural context of San Francisco, the Bay Area, and California was people of all colors—black, brown, red, white, yellow, and everything in between. A popular reason given for the current demand for ethnic studies from elementary to college education is the changing demographics of California and the United States, from a predominantly White and Black nation to what Jesse Jackson coined in his 1988 presidential campaign "the Rainbow Coalition." But in 1968, in San Francisco specifically and California generally, there were already children of every hue of the rainbow. I call them "The Golden Children."

Golden Children, People of Color

The reality is that the children of California were golden long before the Gold Rush of 1849, a precipitating factor in California being admitted to the United States as the 31st state on September 9, 1850. Children were red, brown, yellow, mulatto, mestizo, black, and white. As part of Native America and then Spanish America and Mexican territory, San Francisco was earlier known as Yerba Buena and before that as Yelamu, home to the Ramaytush Ohlone Indians. The people of color of California, the Golden Children, were not children of immigrants but,

---

3   C. Matt Schudel, "Appreciation for Jim Vance," *SFGate*, July 22, 2017.

rather, in the case of American Indians and Latinos, the descendants of indigenous people who preceded the White Anglo Saxon Protestants, the White Americans. Black people were kidnapped slaves from Africa, not immigrants. Similarly, Filipinos, Puerto Ricans, and Pacific Islanders were former Spanish colonies subjected to new US colonization by the Spanish-American war in the late 19th century. These brown Asians and Afro-indigenous Latinos entered the United States initially as nationals. Other brown Asians from the 20th century war of aggression by the US in Laos, Vietnam, and Cambodia entered as refugees, not immigrants.

In addition to recognizing that Third World peoples arrived in the United States primarily due to American wars initiated in their home lands, an equally notable but not readily acknowledged reason is that people of the Third World arrived in the United States because of the labor needs of the United States.[4] This economic exploitation first occurred when African peoples were kidnapped and enslaved to cultivate an economy of tobacco and cotton in hot and humid Jamestown, VA and the South, which were unfamiliar living and agricultural terrains for the white Anglo Saxons. Without support from American Indians and African slaves, the white refugees would have perished. Post-slavery labor in the West consisted of Chinese, Japanese, and Filipino workers from across the Pacific and Mexican braceros and workers from across the Rio Grande, which resulted in rich agricultural and fishery bounty, first in Hawaii and then from California to Alaska. The Chinese were recruited initially as temporary laborers to build the transcontinental railroad. After all, the Chinese had built the Great Wall of China. The Japanese, Chinese, Filipinos, Puerto Ricans and Portuguese were also recruited as short-term contract laborers for Hawaiian sugar cane plantations. While the United States is imagined as the North and South, the free and the slave, it is the East-West divide which better explains the Golden Children. East of the Mississippi, the color line is Black and White. West of the Mississippi it is White and non-White. The colors of the West since the founding of the US are red, brown, yellow, black and white. It is the

---

4 Lucie Cheng Hirata and Edna Bonacich, *Labor Immigration under Capitalism; Asian Workers in the United States before World War I*, (Berkeley, University of California Press, 1984).

rainbow with the golden pot at its end.

The founding of the United Nations in San Francisco also reinforced a cultural view beyond Black and White. Representatives of fifty original member nations signed the Charter of the United Nations on June 26, 1945. It was written in various languages in addition to English—Arabic, Chinese, French, Russian and Spanish. As a reminder of this historic occasion, the flags of member countries of the UN are flown in front of the Fairmont Hotel on San Francisco's Nob Hill.

In recent years, the organic multicultural, multilingual and global context of the San Francisco Bay Area has been eloquently articulated by National Park Ranger Betty Reid Soskin of the Rosie the Riveter Museum in Richmond, CA. Born in September 1921, Ranger Betty reminds us how in Richmond, CA, Henry Kaiser and men and women of all colors built over 700 ships in two and a half years for World War II. While discrimination certainly did not disappear overnight, this experiment and experience allowed entry of working class folks into the middle class and allowed women to work outside the home or other people's homes. Also shipyard work was urban, not rural and agricultural. It brought different people together, united in a common mission. Different experiences, different perspectives, and different truths co-existed among old and new neighbors. Ranger Betty noted that visionaries come from San Francisco; folks come from other parts of the US and other countries come to visit and sometimes stay to be part of many creative visions.[5]

The children of California were the children of the rainbow long before the 21st century, when today, so much is made about states where people of color are not in the majority. What was striking in post-world War II California was that the Golden Children in San Francisco lived primarily in neighborhoods segregated by ethnicity and race. These included the Western Addition (notably the Fillmore/Japantown), the Mission, Hunter's Point/Bayview and Chinatown. Many of the San Francisco State student strikers, including leaders, had grown up in the segregated neighborhoods of San Francisco and were products of the Catholic Church (and parochial schools), which ministered to immigrant

---

5 Betty Reid Soskin (presentation, Aquatic Park Senior Center, San Francisco, CA, May 24, 2017).

and working class communities. In the 19th century, they were mainly Italian and Irish. In the early and mid-20th century, based on labor needs of the West Coast, they included Mexicans, Filipinos, Japanese, Chinese, and Black people migrating from the South and east of the Mississippi, and American Indians migrating from reservations to urban areas. A good number of strikers were imbued with the church's sense of social justice. As a six-year old in 1954, I felt I was in the right place at the right time. I was in first grade at Morning Star School, a Catholic mission school founded by the Society of the Divine Word (SVD) missionaries of Japan. The priests were German and spoke Japanese, English, and Latin, as well as German. They administered the school and offered mass at St. Francis Xavier Church, across the street from Morning Star on Octavia and Pine Streets (now Stuart Hall Boys High School). The nuns were mainly Irish immigrants, belonging to the Belgian order of the Daughters of Mary and Joseph. Father William Stoecke was noted for ministering to his Japanese and Japanese American congregation while they were interned with the 120,000 West Coast residents of Japanese ancestry in prison camps during World War II. During the war, Father Stoecke opened the school to the neighboring children—whites, blacks, Mexicans, Filipinos, American Indians (given the 1950s urban relocation program of American Indians), and the interracial children of US World War II soldiers and their war brides. As a first grader, the first president I met was a black woman—Mrs. Anderson, the mother of my classmate Lunelle, who was the PTA president. While the Catholic faith bound this diverse Morning Star community, which also included many Buddhists, the sense of patriotism was also a strong unifier in the city. We were Americans with multilingual, multicultural, global and ecumenical perspectives and traditions. In my Japantown home, one could hear relatives and visitors conversing in Ilocano, Tagalog, Visayan, Spanish, English, and Japanese. Our fathers were World War II veterans. As a consequence of this military and other patriotic service, citizenship exclusion laws were overturned for Asians and American Indians in the late 1940s and early 1950s. Catholic immigrants and veterans of color from the Third World as well as Southern and Eastern Europe embraced American citizenship, patriotism, and the right to vote.

Jeff Chan, a fellow student striker at San Francisco State and one of the first tenured professors of Asian American Studies, commented on growing up in San Francisco at a similar time, "My earliest memories are of North Beach Chinatown, Catholic daycare, catechism at St. Peter and Paul, of Latin mass, of days of abstinence, of rosaries, solariums, a Chinatown crèche that stuck around till Chinese New year with baby Jesus looking vaguely like my just born cousin Phyllis, the layering aromas of roasting coffee, tomato sauce melding over a low flame, rank cheese, and the smell of *salami* and sawdust in Guido's deli on the corner where I bought my penny candy on my way home from Jean Parker (School), still under an awning that sheltered the boys' yard from the construction dust of the Broadway Tunnel. So it was that I was imbued with a Catholic sensibility until age seven, the Jesuit requirement, and am forever bound.[6] Other fellow strikers and early faculty of the College of Ethnic Studies, San Francisco State were Malcolm Collier and Dan Gonzales who noted, "On a certain level, the Asian American students of the time were following the footsteps of their own parents and communities. When Chinese and Filipino American men worked hard and long enough to raise the funds to bring wives and family from Asia after World War II, they were laying a very emphatic claim to a permanent place in America. However conservative some of their political views may have been (some were quite extreme in their conservatism!), they knew about the struggles of their predecessors as well as their own. They were asserting their rights and challenging the old order by establishing families, seeking new avenues of employment, and moving into neighborhoods where the land was still covered by racial covenants meant to exclude them. They too were concerned with equity and inclusion. Some went further by forming and joining labor unions, and taking public stances on community issues. Seen in the context of this dynamic, it is not at all surprising that many of their children were concerned and active as well."[7]

---

6 Jeff Chan and Scilla Finetti, "Prego," *At 40: Asian American Studies @ San Francisco State*, (San Francisco, Thomson-Shore Inc., 2009), 166.
7 Malcolm Collier and Daniel Phil Gonzales, "Origins: People, Time, Place and Dreams," *At 40: Asian American Studies @ San Francisco State*, (San Francisco, Thomson-Shore Inc., 2009), 10.

From a geographical perspective, San Francisco on a peninsula also solidified a sense of identity and unity. Donna Amador explained part of the Right Place portion of "Being in the Right Place at the Right Time" to SF State Ethnic Studies professor, Jason Ferreira. "In the Bay Area, or at least in San Francisco, people lived right next door to each other. I mean, its (sic) not like Los Angeles where there is: here is West L.A., here is Compton, Watts, and then here is East L.A., way out here. I mean, they didn't mix in the same way, they don't go to school together, they don't live together, they don't shop for groceries together. Most of the people that I was close to in the Third World Liberation Front at State, for instance, a lot of them I had gone to school with, or went to City College with. I mean, in San Francisco, even if somebody lived in the Fillmore and somebody lived in the Mission, in terms of high schools, there just weren't that many and people tended to, at least, know each other casually. It wasn't like barriers existed. So, a lot of folks just knew each other, and when you know somebody, it's really easy to say 'Hey, I'm gonna do this, come on, let's go do it together.' It's not like strangers. And I think in the Bay Area, there was a lot more of that going on. I don't think that it is as easy in many other places, you have to go out of your way. I don't think we needed to do that."[8] Ferreira's larger point was that a Third World consciousness by young radicals like Amador was influenced by their daily lives as people of color who at least knew of one another.

It is only in recent years with various milestones—such as the San Francisco Giants victories in the 2010, 2012 and 2014 World Series, the centennial anniversary of the San Francisco Municipal Railway in 2012, and the 50th anniversary of the 1967 Summer of Love in 2017—that the idea of being in the right place at the right time to allow for a successful student-led strike and the first and most enduring College of Ethnic Studies has sunk in.

Ten years before the San Francisco State strike, San Francisco children were thrilled to go to Seals Stadium in 1958 (then later to

---

8 Jason Michael Ferreira, "All Power to the People: A Comparative History of Third World Radicalism in San Francisco, 1969-1974," PhD diss., (University of California, Berkeley, 2003), 283.

Candlestick Park) to watch the San Francisco Giants play major league baseball, especially against the Los Angeles Dodgers. We no longer just had comics and television heroes. We could root for and get our baseball cards autographed by real-live heroes and role models—Willie Mays, Willy McCovey, Juan Marichal, Orlando Cepeda, and the Alou brothers, Felipe, Jesus and Mateo, among others. With both Jackie Robinson's historic entry in 1947 as the first black player in the major leagues with the Brooklyn Dodgers and the move of major league baseball out West, we could root for heroes who looked like us. But the reality that we were still second-class citizens hit us when Willie Mays was barred from buying a home in the exclusive St. Francis Woods neighborhood because he was Black; because he was not white. This was an important early life lesson for children of veterans and citizens of the United States who were not white.

Despite segregated neighborhoods, the children of San Francisco could ride the San Francisco Municipal Railway all over town to see the other parts of the city. At a cost of five cents a ride with transfers (a student bus card costing fifty cents for ten rides), we could explore Playland at the Beach as well as the Ferry Building and go off to McLaren Park then pass through City Hall, the San Francisco Main Library and Civic Center on the way to Fisherman's Wharf and Baker Beach. We could ride through the neighborhoods of rich whites in Pacific Heights and Nob Hill where our dads were janitors, bus boys, waiters and bartenders, and detour through hippie Haight Ashbury before going home to Chinatown, Bernal Heights, Bayview, or Hunter's Point. We rode the buses not only to the baseball stadiums but to City College of San Francisco and San Francisco State College and even the Haight Ashbury.

The popular story of the Haight Ashbury is about the Summer of Love in 1967 when, according to some accounts, over 100,000 young people descended on San Francisco in search of peace, love, and collective and individual freedom. The more sobering story is that due to redevelopment in the Western Addition, many working class residents of color were relocated west from the Fillmore and Japantown to the Haight Ashbury. These young people of color who grew up in the Haight were also involved in the hippie movement. Their role in the politics, arts and music of that period was not as acknowledged as those of white ones. In photo exhibits of *The Summer at Love* in 2017 at the San Francisco City Hall, the San Francisco Main Library, and the De Young Museum in Golden Gate Park, they are barely mentioned. There are a few photos of the Black Panthers and musicians such as Jimi Hendrix and Santana. Yet, the very public and unconventional expressions of peace and end to the Vietnam War and the draft with respect for the planet resonated not just with white youth but children of color. After all, young men of color, lower income and not college-educated, like the young men of Central City, the Mission, the Fillmore and Chinatown, were disproportionately drafted for and fought in the Vietnam War. The enemies in Southeast Asia—Vietnam Laos, Cambodia—had common ancestry with Asian Americans—Chinese, Japanese, Korean, Filipino. Asian American soldiers were mistaken as "gooks."

The De Young Museum exhibit was titled, "San Francisco's Love Generation: The Summer of Love Experience." It focused on the art, fashion, and music of the period based on private collections of wealthy donors rather than being a depiction of the thousands of Bay Area and American youth from across the country who were working class and middle class. On one of the walls at the beginning of the exhibit are several quotes. One was from then Assemblyman Willie Brown to the San Francisco Board of Supervisors (a San Francisco State alumnus who went on to be the city's first Black mayor), "If you declare against these young people today what minority is going to bear the brunt of your discrimination tomorrow?"

The San Francisco Main Library exhibit "Summer of Love and Haight" was more expansive and inclusive including: artifacts from the media, the drug culture, information about then Governor Ronald Reagan, social movements (including a section on the SF state strike) and photos of Asian, Latino, Black, and white children in their neighborhoods. It also made note of the reclamation of Alcatraz in 1969 by some one hundred Native Americans, many of whom came from San Francisco State, including Richard Oakes. This exhibit noted that this phenomenon of mainly white disenchanted youth from the heartland challenging the conforming culture of the 1950s was the beginning of the Rust Belt as documented in *We Are the People our Parents Warned Us about* by Nicholas Hoffman. The exhibit's section on "Sex, Drugs and Runaways and Haight-Ashbury's Summer of Love: National and Local Media Coverage" featured *Love Needs Care*, 1970 authored by Dr. David E. Smith (with John Luce) founder of the Haight-Ashbury Free Clinic. The power of the Free Clinic was to heal unconditionally and compassionately the youth of the nation who left or ran away from home to look for the dawning of Aquarius—for peace, love, and social justice in the City of St. Francis.

Ben Fong-Torres, a San Francisco State alumnus and famous *Rolling Stone* magazine *and San Francisco Chronicle* journalist, was one of the first few people of color to document the hippie counterculture, especially in terms of music. He studied broadcasting and journalism at San Francisco State and in 1967 as a 22-year-old, was a deejay on KFOG, which was then considered a "beautiful, easy-listening music" station. With the coming of the hippies, he was able to pivot and capture the variety of music of new local bands such as Jerry Garcia's Grateful Dead and Grace Slick and the Jefferson Airplane. In an interview with Rachel Myrow, Fong-Torres noted that the music of the counterculture was not just entertainment but filled with community-oriented messages:

> Myrow: What was it about the music—the Grateful Dead, Big Brother and the Holding Company, Jefferson Airplane—that was so appealing?

> Fong-Torres: Sometimes, it wasn't the music. Sometimes, it was the sense of community that the bands were the epicenters of. It wasn't as if there was a San Francisco sound, or psychedelic rock. Each band had various members who came from their own musical bands and interests. So, it could be folk or classical. It could be jazz or blues. It could be country. All of it was welcomed into whatever the repertoire was of the band, as long as the other people dug it and could play it. Even if they couldn't, they would learn how to do it. A lot of bands were formed for the fun of it, including people who hadn't played those instruments.

Myrow: Were there people who believed at that time that rock music would save the world?

Fong-Torres: By then, because of Bob Dylan and other folk musicians, we were hearing messages in music. Sometimes, of course, music can be a gel. It can be a binding force, a rallying cry. "We shall overcome."

I think more and more young people began to see music and hear music as something more than pop songs on the radio. They became, really, a soundtrack to this emerging counterculture: not just a culture, but specifically, a counterculture.[9]

In his autobiography, *Rice Room*, Ben juxtaposed his life as participant-observer in the counterculture to that of his brother, Barry, who chose to work directly with disaffected youth in the community, particularly Chinese immigrant, non-English-speaking males. Barry Fong-Torres was the director of the Youth Services Coordinating Center in Chinatown, working with young men and women not that different from the ones at St Patrick Youth Center in Central City. He was gunned down at 29 years of age for his brave but unwelcomed interventions.

Several San Francisco radio stations in the late 1950s and 1960s were attractive to non-traditional audiences, including teenagers. KSFO AM covered the San Francisco Giants with Russ Hodges and Lon Simmons and, for adult audiences, provided witty deejays such as Don Sherwood, Dan Sorkin, and Jim Lange. For young Baby Boomers—then the new teenage audience—their stations were KEWB and KYA Boss of the Bay with Gene Nelson, Tom Donohue, and Russ "The Moose" Syracuse. Top 40 radio disc jockey KYA (1260 AM) in August 1966, promoted and hosted the last live concert performance by The Beatles, at wind-swept Candlestick Park. In 1965, Johnny Holliday was America's number one disc jockey. These stations played not only rock and roll songs by white musicians but folk and protest songs, such as "Blowing in the Wind" and "Where Have All the Flowers Gone." They also featured

---

9 Ben Fong-Torres, "Ben Fong-Torres Remembers His Summer of Love in San Francisco," interview by Rachel Myrow. *KQED*, July 7, 2017.

crossover songs by Black musicians including Chuck Berry, Sam Cooke, and the stars of Motown. Johnny Mathis was hailed as a hometown celebrity, graduating from Washington High School and San Francisco State. The stations also had latitude to introduce best-selling hits by foreigners such as "Dominque" by Belgian singing nun, Soeur Sourire, "Sukiyaki," sung by Japanese musician Kyu Sakamoto, and "The Girl from Ipanema," sung in English by Astrud Gilberto and in Portuguese by Joao Gilberto. "La Bamba" became a top 40s hit song in Spanish by a Mexican American teenager from Los Angeles named Richie Valens (Valenzuela). In addition, stations played music by local multiracial groups such as Santana from the Mission and Sly and the Family Stone from Vallejo. The latter featured young women and men, many of them related. As musician Tom Petty noted to in a 2006 "Fresh Air" interview with Terry Gross, in the 1960s, there was literacy in music, open to all, and not compartmentalized. The world was big. The deejays were brave. In 1965, as teenagers, we heard Buffy Sainte-Marie's "Universal Solider" and Barry McGuire's "Eve of Destruction" over and over again. By 1969, sweet, joyful, hopeful music, labeled as cross-over music, such as "Oh, Happy Day" by the Edwin Hawkins Singers played all over Bay Area radio stations

These explicit and implicit elements of history and culture acknowledged the existence and experience of peoples of color—Third World peoples—in the United States. Taken together, they facilitated the birth and success of a student-led strike at San Francisco State in 1968 and the establishment of the School of Ethnic Studies.

A Master Plan for Higher Education in California, 1960 -1975

Since 1790, racial segregation and subordination has been the policy of the United States. It is embedded in the Constitution and was reflected in the decennial census of the population.[10] The impact of these policies were pervasive and continue today. Over time, it included kidnapped Black Africans sold as chattel slaves under British colonial rule; the Indian Wars perpetrated by European colonists and later, by Canadian

---

10   Margo Anderson, *The American Census: A Social History*, (New Haven, Yale University Press, 1988), 9 and 12.

and American governments, that seized ownership of lands traditionally inhabited by indigenous peoples; the Chinese Exclusion Act of 1882; the late 19th century Manifest Destiny doctrine whereby the United States seized the Philippines, Hawaii and Puerto Rico; and, during World War II, the internment of Japanese Americans as foreign enemies. In 2018, the latest victims of this legacy of white supremacy are "the Dreamers," young people, primarily of Latino descent, brought to the United States by parents without documentation, and Black and brown people, primarily young, killed without due process by police officers and other extrajudicial actors.

Segregation and subordination is also the historical tradition of the American educational system. It was only with the 1954 Supreme Court case, *Brown v. the Board of Education*, that public elementary and secondary schools were desegregated. In higher education, San Francisco State and other colleges and universities led the way in the late 1960s and early 1970s in ensuring access to higher education for not only people of color, but also for women and other traditionally underrepresented groups, including rural and low income students.

For Black people, most historically Black colleges and universities were established after the Civil War with the assistance of northern religious missionary organizations. Exceptions included Lincoln University in Lincoln University, PA, the first degree-granting historically Black university in the US, founded in 1854 by Presbyterian minister John Miller Dickey and his wife, Sarah Emlen Cresson, a Quaker. The Morrill Act of 1890, also known as the Agricultural College Act of 1890, established land grant colleges specifically for Black people if they were excluded from existing land grant colleges, in locations notably but not only in the South. The Higher Education Act of 1965 established a program for direct federal grants to historically Black colleges and universities. These colleges and universities provided a traditional education and produced twentieth century Black human capital and leadership. In his 2015 article on the relevance of Black colleges today, Alexander Nazaryan noted, "And while HBCUs account for only 3 percent of the nation's colleges, they account for about 20 percent of the degrees awarded to African-

Americans."[11] With respect to American Indians, segregation was initially via reservations. In the late 19th and early 20th centuries, however, there was a move to assimilate American Indian children into Euro-American culture. This was accomplished via The Civilization Funding Act of 1819. American Indian boarding schools were set up. First run by white Christian missionaries, they were subsequently institutionalized by the Bureau of Indian Affairs. Children were separated from their families, forbidden to speak their native languages, and disciplined to assimilate to Euro-American mannerisms and dress. Boarding schools were sometimes far from their home reservations. Carlisle Indian Industrial School in Carlisle, PA was the most well-known Indian boarding school from 1879–1918. Only in the 1980s, with the rise of pan-Indian activism such as the strike at San Francisco State and other campuses and the fight for the passage of the Indian Self-Determination and Education Assistance Act of 1975, did boarding schools close in large numbers.

The educational segregation of Asian Americans occurred on the West Coast with a 1906 policy by the San Francisco School Board mandating students of Asian descent—Chinese, Korean, and Japanese—attend the Oriental School on Clay Street in Chinatown. Only in 2017 was this segregation policy repealed.[12]

Mexican Americans also attended segregated schools with schools designated as "whites only" and "Mexican." Before the *Brown v. Board of Education*, 1954 Supreme Court case, the *Mendez v. Westminster* case in 1947 successfully challenged the segregation of Mexican American students in Orange County, CA. Five Mexican American fathers—Thomas Estrada, William Guzman, Gonzalo Mendez, Frank Palomino, and Lorenzo Ramirez—brought suit in the United States District Court for the Central District in Los Angeles. Using some of the arguments in *Mendez*, the *Brown* case had thirteen parents—notably Reverend Oliver L. Brown, Darlene Brown, Lena Carper, Sadie Emmanuel, Marguerite Emerson, Shirley Fleming, Zelma Henderson, Shirley Hodison, Maude Lawton, Alma Lewis, Iona Richardson, and Lucinda Todd—file suit on

---

11   Alexander Nazaryan, "Black Colleges Matter," *Newsweek*, August 18, 2015.
12   Jill Tucker, "SF School Board to Repeal Old Rule Segregating Asian Students," *San Francisco Chronicle*, January 23, 2017.

behalf of their twenty children.

Many of the above examples of systematic racial segregation and subordination throughout the history of the United States, and specifically in California, were not necessarily known in 1968–1969, except on an ad hoc basis. Rather, they have come to light as pieces of a larger puzzle through the establishment of ethnic studies scholarship and programs and other post-1960s institutions. The shift toward a more inclusive narrative of the peoples of the United States blossomed after the various movements of the 1960s.

From the perspective of children growing up in San Francisco in the 1950s, this historical segregation was not as obvious. The Golden Children of California were growing as a proportion of the state population, not as temporary residents, but as permanent residents and citizens, and oftentimes as offspring of military veterans and naturalized citizens. They were here to stay. While they lived in ethnically and racially segregated neighborhoods, schools in a few neighborhoods were not as starkly segregated as in the South. Class photos indicate a rainbow of children, such as a Raphael Weill Elementary class photo circa 1930s in the San Francisco Main Library History Center. Moreover, in the 1950s, SF State and City College of San Francisco had a sizable number of non-white students, especially Black students, then called Negroes. Thus, when the student-led strike occurred at SF. State, the impetus was organic, not abstract nor academic. It was driven by students and the needs of the larger community beyond the college.

As captured by William Barlow and Peter Shapiro:

"While the Free Speech Movement was taking place at Berkeley, students across the bay at San Francisco State College were quietly engaging in an unpublicized struggle of their own. The ultimate stakes were the same but the milieu could not have been more different. Instead of a nationally renowned ivory tower, it consisted of a drab, unimpressive-looking "streetcar college" which had been designated for mediocrity by the Master Plan for higher education. Owing to its location in a city which has traditionally been a center of radical politics and cultural ferment, it had attracted some outstanding professors and a generally intelligent, independent-minded student body. Its strongest departments were in the humanities and creative arts; its faculty liked to think of itself as of university caliber. But the atmosphere on campus was deceptively low-keyed. College governance was entrusted to a remote, rigid, and notoriously unwieldy statewide administrative bureaucracy whose main concern was keeping operating costs at a bare minimum. For the moment, it was singularly indifferent to the activities of the students in its charge, and rather than reacting against the anonymity as their Berkeley counterparts had done, student activists at S.F. State were able to use it to their advantage as they labored toward a new definition of their education, more in line with their own interests, priorities, and values.[13]

"The period from 1964 to 1966 saw an entire generation of college students become educated in radical politics. At S.F. State, this educational process took place at its greatest intensity and assumed a form that was completely unprecedented for the time and is not likely to be repeated in the future. The 'form' was that of the 'student programs'; initiated by student activists with the aid and encouragement of sympathetic faculty and lower level administrators, the programs evolved in an atmosphere of relative serenity and campus harmony, and within a few years they had become the pride of the college. Still, and despite their atypical nature, they bore an organic relationship to a particular phase of the student movement in the United States, and by living out the phase under optimum conditions, student activists at S.F. State were able to develop some of the best, most committed most politically sophisticated radical leadership on any campus in the country. Beginning with the Fillmore Tutorial, the programs had by 1966 expanded to include the Community Involvement Program, the Work-

---

13   William Barlow and Peter Shapiro, *An End to Silence: the San Francisco State Student Movement in the 60s*, (New York, Pegasus, 1971), 56-57.

Study Program, and the much-heralded Experimental College before their major impetus and organization model were taken by the Black Student Union."[14]

Embedded in these radical programs was the value of education relevant to the working class citizens of San Francisco and California. The mission of public schools in a representative democracy was to ensure an informed, civic-minded population and a competent, educated workforce. Many communities knew that education was the access route for people born without wealth, privilege and legacy. Especially for a post-industrial, globally-competitive economy, strong human capital was imperative for California. Like other states, California in the 1950s experienced a growth in population, including college enrollment by servicemen taking advantage of the GI Bill following World War II and the Korean War. "By 1957, when the wave of GIs had more or less subsided, the war babies were just reaching college age, and a new wave of entering freshmen pushed enrollment figures even higher."[15] With the draft for the Vietnam War, young men applied for exemptions, including college deferments.

Competition for seats in college became a challenge. The state of California responded to this challenge with the development of the Master Plan for Higher Education in California, 1960–1976.[16]

> "An amendment be proposed to add a new section to Article IX of the California Constitution providing that: Public higher education shall consist of the junior colleges, the State College System, and the University of California. Each shall strive for excellence in its sphere, as assigned in this section.

> "The junior colleges shall be governed by local boards selected for the purpose from each district maintaining one or more junior colleges. The State Board of Education shall prescribe minimum standards for the formation and operation of junior

---

14   Ibid., 57-58.
15   Ibid., 25.
16   Arthur G. Coons, *A Master Plan for Higher Education in California, 1960-1975*, (Sacramento, California State Department of Education, 1960).

colleges, and shall exercise general supervision over said junior colleges, as prescribed by law. Said public junior colleges shall offer instruction through but not beyond the fourteenth-grade level including, but courses not for limited to, one or more of the following: (a) standard collegiate transfer to higher institutions, (b) vocational-technical fields leading to employment, and (c) general, or liberal arts courses. Studies in these fields may lead to the Associate in Arts or Associate in Science degree. Nothing in this section shall be construed as altering the status of the junior college as part of the Public School System as defined elsewhere in the Constitution

"The state colleges shall have as their primary function the provision of instruction in the liberal arts and sciences and in professions and applied fields which require more than two years of collegiate education and teacher education, both for undergraduate students and graduate students through the master's degree. The doctoral degree may be awarded jointly with the University of California, as hereinafter provided. Faculty research, using facilities provided for and consistent with the primary function of the state colleges, is authorized.

"The University of California shall be governed by The Regents as provided in Section 9 of Article IX of the California Constitution. The University shall provide instruction in the liberal arts and sciences, and in the professions, including teacher education, and shall have exclusive jurisdiction over training for the professions (including but not by way of limitation) dentistry, law, medicine, veterinary medicine, and graduate architecture. The University shall have the sole authority in public higher education to award the doctor's degree in all fields of learning, except that it may agree with the state colleges to award joint doctor's degrees in selected fields. The University shall be the primary state-supported academic agency for research, and The Regents shall make reasonable provision for the use of its library and research facilities by qualified members of the faculties of other higher educational institutions, public and private.

"The two governing boards reaffirm the long established principle that state colleges and the University of California shall be tuition free to all residents of the state."

Junior colleges as part of public school system were also tuition-free. The report went on to describe the growing California population:

"The causes of this projected increase in college enrollments are easy to determine. By the end of World War II, the birth rate in California had increased by 50 per cent over that of prewar days and has remained near this level. Added to the birth rate increase has been a continued large scale inmigration. This influx of population is expected to show net gains of 300,000 or more annually in the years ahead. According to current estimates of the State Department of Finance California's population was 15,280,000 on July 1, 1959, and is expected to increase to over 25,000,000 by 1975. By the year 2020, this state is expected to contain 58,000,000 persons, nearly four times its present population."

Just as the United States was emerging as a world-class leader, California was also growing demographically and economically. Its human capital was the engine of growth. The University of California was viewed as a "public trust." Free public education from elementary school to university demonstrated that California's priority was its children, its human capital. Before the master plan, college presidents appealed directly to state legislature for funds; 70% of high school graduates were eligible to be admitted to state colleges; the top 33% to university. Corporations paid only 20% of tax burden.

In order to implement the master plan, the state did not increase taxes, particularly corporate ones. Instead, it modified who could obtain higher education. Centralized under the governor and his political appointees—Trustees, Regents, and Coordinating council—most of whom were representatives for big business—tracking was implemented in public schools. The three-prong higher education system channeled high school graduates to junior colleges supported by local taxes. The top 12.5 % of high school graduates were eligible to apply to the university; the top 33% to state colleges. The impact on San Francisco State was notable. Enrollment of Black students declined over 10 years (1959–1969) from 10% to 3%. The nonwhite enrollment dropped from 12% to 3% at SF State after tracking and SAT requirements were introduced. During this period, nonwhite students increased their proportion in San Francisco public schools at almost 50%.[17]

The master plan was a volatile and contentious way of distributing education for the "public good." The exclusion of a potentially large and necessary source of human capital did not sit well with the Golden Children, whose parents, forefathers, and foremothers had created and contributed to California. They were the working class and middle class majority. Students like the leaders of Third World Liberation Front would not stand for their younger siblings and cousins to be excluded. Fellow students, faculty, staff, and the larger community would not allow for the exclusion of the next generation of permanent residents, citizens, and labor force into public higher education. Coming together as family, community, and neighbors, their tradition was to honor those who came before them and nurture those who came after. Their collective experience in California and the United States was that power could be coercive or collective.

For the Golden Children and their families, the strike at San Francisco State and the fight for ethnic studies was a fight for inclusion, representation, and participation in higher education. Education was not just the key to knowledge and to the mainstream but also to self-determination. It was the fight for education that acknowledged and was relevant to their lives and futures. But more basically, the golden children were stewards and witnesses. Their stewardship was honoring the legacy of their ancestors and serving the needs of current and future generations. Their witness was to verify and document their vital

---

17 Oakland Community Support Committee for SF State, "The Decline of Our State Colleges and the 1959-60 Master Plan for Higher Education," SF State Strike Archives, Sharon Martinas Collection, Box 1, folder 13.

presence to San Francisco, California, and the United States. They were willing to go on strike, lose coveted student, staff, and faculty positions, be deported, and even go to jail. Many of them remain unsung heroes and heroines. They were in the right place at the right time.

GOLDEN CHILDREN

CHAPTER 2

Practical Grassroots Origins: Unsung Heroines and Heroes

In reviewing the literature and media coverage on the 1968–1969 student strike at San Francisco State and the establishment of the School of Ethnics Studies that were produced during, or shortly after, these events, what glaringly stands out is the invisibility of the everyday people. What is missing is the working class youth, children, and adults who actually went on strike and who took on the tasks of negotiating the strike settlement, dealing with the aftermath of arrests, and putting together the actual nuts and bolts of establishing a new institution that had never before existed in the history of higher education in the United States. This is not insignificant. Today, after 50 years, the College of Ethnic Studies at San Francisco State is the only ethnic studies program in the nation and the world. While other universities, especially elite universities, host their rock star ethnic studies professors and special programs, no other institution of higher education has a full college with a dean, several departments, majors, minors, budget and building. No other ethnic studies program highlights social justice and serving the everyday needs of everyday people as its core mission. Community service is still integral to students of ethnic studies at San Francisco State.

As noted in the introduction, it was only in 2009 that the leaders of the 1968–1969 Third World Strike at San Francisco State were formally recognized and honored. There are several reasons why the San Francisco State students went unrecognized for decades.

Non-recognition for decades
One reason is that the leadership was dispersed across several student organizations that comprised the TWLF Central Committee. The position of chair and spokespersons rotated across the organizations. This fluidity and de-centralization was purposive. Penny Nakatsu, a member of the TWLF Central Committee, the Asian American Political

Alliance, and the Asian American Studies Planning Committee noted that hundreds of students supported the BSU/TWLF strike and were willing to demonstrate, speak up, and even be arrested for freedom of speech and lawful assembly. Penny also noted that dozens of students, along with faculty and community representatives on their own time, participated in many planning groups and committees that developed the ethnic studies curriculum. Other strikers and supporters of ethnic studies echoed Nakatsu's comment. The work and sacrifices individually and collectively of many persons led to the birth of the ethnic studies program.[1] In my view, as noted below, while the students were in the vanguard, the success of this historic strike and establishment of the College of Ethnic Studies was dependent on continuing support from local Bay Area neighborhoods and the wider communities.

Second, the TWLF leaders and strikers respected the traditional cultures of their families, communities, and religions, where the whole is greater than the sum of its parts and certainly greater than any individual. No one person shines. The collective, the group, was more important than any ego. Third World cultures colonized by the First World of Western Europe and North America cultures could only survive as a united group. Hence, the popular slogan during this period, "A people united can never be defeated" echoed amongst Third World revolutionaries in Africa, Asia, and Latin America and protest movements in the United States and Western Europe. As Eddie Williams, founding director of DC-based Black think tank, The Joint Center for Political and Economic Studies, used to caution young people of color as they left their post-strike campuses and traveled to Washington, DC to be interns or employees, "We either hang together, or hang separately."

From the traditional faith cultures of honoring Mother Earth to the colonized ones of intercession through Jesus or his mother, Mary, a faith based in service and humility was emphasized in communities

---

1   Penny Nakatsu, personal communication with author, November 5, 2016. See also, "40th Anniversary of the 1968 SF State Black Student Union/Third World Liberation Front Student-led Strike," *The SF State College Strike Collection*, https://diva.sfsu.edu/collections/coes/9191, and "Interview," https://diva.sfsu.edu/collections/coes/9192.

of color, especially amongst immigrant Asian American and Latino communities. They were taught to honor their elders who had sacrificed so much so they could have a better life, partake of the American dream, and be the first in their families to attend and graduate from college in the United States. In 1968, many people of color and white women were still pioneers and numerical minorities, the first in their families to gain access to college, long the bastion of privileged upper class white males. They were invisible and often quiet.

Third, the TWLF leadership was composed of men and women who could check their egos at the door (the leadership was mainly men). They had been leaders in grammar and high school and learned to serve. For the most part, they were self-effacing without big egos while commanding respect and admiration on campus and in their communities.[2] Roger Alvarado comes to mind as a prime example. He was also an active and early supporter of the 2016 TWLF strikers on campus. While some of the 1968–1969 leaders were teenagers or in their twenties, there were a few adults seasoned by life events and service in the military, such as Mason Wong, who had served in the Marines Corps and was president of Intercollegiate Chinese for Social Action. Al Wong, TWLF Central Committee Chair and Nesbitt Crutchfield of the BSU Central Committee had served in the Air Force. They had been in combat in Vietnam or the Cold War.[3] Moreover, several of the TWLF Central Committee were children of leaders in their communities, including pastors of local churches. For example, Benny Stewart's father was a minister. Danny Glover's parents, Carrie and James Glover, were leaders in the local Negro community organizations and the NAACP (National Association from the Advancement of Colored People) founded in 1909 by W.E.B. Du Bois. Rich Wada's father, Yoritada Wada, was the executive director of the Buchanan Street YMCA in the Fillmore/Japantown/ Western Addition. He has been credited for decades of work advocating for youth from various ethnic neighborhoods, not just among Black

---

2   Daniel Gonzales, interview, *The SF State College Strike Collection*, https://diva. sfsu.edu/collections/coes/bundles/ 218201.
3   "The Straight Story," *The SF State College Strike Collection*, https://diva.sfsu. edu/collections/coes/bundles/218242.

people and Asian Americans.[4] My father, Lazaro Lorenzo Tamayo, was an officer and founding member of the International Family Circle started in 1940 in San Francisco. While members were mainly from the Filipino American community, the circle's vision was global citizenship on the brink of World War II. Its logo was a circle or globe. This vision was quite remarkable for the period, as the Philippines was still a commonwealth, a transitional stage from being a colony of the United States in 1935 to an independent republic in 1946. Hence during this interim, Filipino Americans were neither nationals nor citizens but aliens. Nonetheless, the TWLF and its supporters covered the range of aliens, nationals, immigrants and citizens.

Fourth, an advantage of the TWLF leaders, members, and supporters is that they were local with deep roots in the Bay Area and California over generations. They were from the 'hood. Many had attended San Francisco public and parochial elementary and high schools. People knew one another, or at least knew of their families from working class and racial/ethnic neighborhoods. They were commuters, homeboys and homegirls not necessarily looking for or wanting external validation. This was a distinction from the White youth of SDS or organizations of people of color at UC Berkeley or Cornell, where significant portions of the students were temporary out-of-town and out-of-state residents.

Given the three-tier structure of the master plan for higher education in California, the University of California students tended to be upper middle class, including the minority students, as opposed to the state university students, who were from the middle class and working class. Valerie Anthony observed and compared both San Francisco State and the University of California, Berkeley, campuses during their respective strikes with a rich journal for her SF State Speech Department classes on semantics and social control. Coming from an upper-class white background, Anthony noted that core values of the upper middle class initially prevented strike participation, which was considered

---

4 Annie Nakao, "Yori Wada, Former UC Regent, Community Leader Dies at 80," *SFGate*, November 18, 1997, http://www.sfgate.com/news/article/Yori-Wada-former-UC-regent-community-leader-3087890.php.

inappropriate for their reference group.[5] During a KQED interview, then interim President Hayakawa, chastised college departmental chairs as irresponsible for encouraging teachers to strike and declared, "this college is not a rich man's college … it's a college in which the children of working class people and the children of immigrants get their chance at a college education."[6]

Fifth, survival skills that children of color learned while growing up in the United States were to not stand out as different according to mainstream society's expectations but blend in the crowd, especially when one is working class. This was taken to the extreme by the Nisei generation, many of whom were the parents to the Sansei strikers on campus. The hard lesson of the internment of Japanese and Japanese Americans during World War II was to be the silent American, to be the model minority while out-whiting Whitey. The strikers knew that their parents and grandparents experienced racial and ethnic discrimination in their Third World countries of origin as colonized or enslaved peoples exploited for natural resources and human capital. They also witnessed what happened to very visible leaders in the Civil Rights Movement and the Black Panther Party. For people of color today, Clint Smith's TED talk, "How to Raise a Black Son"[7] is sobering and not that different from the survival skills learned by the TWLF leaders, members and supporters. As historian Howard Zinn succinctly stated in his November 1970 article, "The Problem is Civil Disobedience," "In every city in this country, when demonstrations take place, the protestors, whether they have demonstrated or not, whatever they have done, are assaulted and clubbed by the police, and then they are arrested for assaulting a police officer."[8]

---

5   Valerie Anthony, "I Believe: San Francisco State College Strike Scrapbook," volume 1, San Francisco Public Library.

6   "Alioto & Hayakawa Press Conference," *The SF State College Strike Collection*, https://diva.sfsu.edu/collections/ strike/bundles/187215.

7   Clint Smith, "How to Raise a Black Son in America," *TED2015*, March 2015, https://www.ted.com/talks/ clint_smith_how_to_raise_a_black_son_in_america.

8   Howard Zinn, "The Problem is Civil Disobedience," http://www.informationclearinghouse.info/article36950.htm.

Sixth, from a Eurocentric framework, or as then Black Studies proposed chairman Professor Nathan Hare and others called the WASP or White Anglo Saxon Protestant perspective, categorizing by hierarchy meant identifying leaders and isolating them. People of color have been categorized by the white power structure—via politicians or the media—as spokespersons or designated leaders, or in the case of WEB DuBois as "race men." Instead of understanding people of color as a diverse body, individuals were singled out to speak for the group or as dissenters inciting protest. Yet, as minorities, people of color were not recognized as leaders outside of their respective communities. People of color were not acknowledged as public leaders on larger public issues or in mainstream positions. In 1968–1969 the concept of persons as individuals via individualism and meritocracy had not taken hold as in 2018–2019. Persons were members of reference groups. There was not yet a disproportionate amount of individualism and meritocracy.

Seventh, SF State was a public state university for middle and working class students. They were second-class citizens to elite public and private universities. They were not part of the establishment nor were they part of media's traditional source for knowledge, innovation or understanding of the needs of everyday people.

Eighth, from a historical perspective, there was a shift in Eurocentric society from a culture of great leaders of World War II, such as Franklin D. Roosevelt and Winston Churchill, to a Western culture of the anti-hero during the 1950s and 1960s. One literary example of the antihero was Captain John Yossarian, an Army Air Force B-26 bombardier, the protagonist in Joseph Heller's satirical novel, *Catch-22*. The National Aeronautical and Space Administration (NASA) epitomized a new order of not one hero but a heroic team. As they prepared for various space missions, the highpoint being the moon landing in 1969, NASA's culture emphasized that everyone was responsible for its missions, from the janitors to astronauts. The GS 13 and 14 astronauts were not celebrities but civil servants. Their strength, sustainability and power were not as individuals but as a team.

Ninth, is that things take time to be acknowledged, remembered, and placed in multiple perspectives, especially if they are life changing events such going to jail, losing a job, or getting deported. My observation from talks with fellow strikers and advocates of ethnic studies through the decades and at various screenings in 2016, 2017 and 2018 of *Agents of Change* was that their experience was very personal and oftentimes hard to objectify or even articulate. So much happened in a relatively short time period. Many could easily have been a quiet hero or heroine.

Examples abound where there is a time lag between a historical event and its documentation or even acknowledgement at a deep level. The reality of experience and the required detachment of reflection takes time. One example is Alex *Haley's Roots: The Saga of an American Family*, a novel about American slavery. Slavery was as old as the British colonies but was not depicted until it debuted as a television mini-series in 1976, during the Bicentennial Year of the United States. In 2017, after more than fifty years, soldiers on both sides of the American War in Southeast Asia have been acknowledged and allowed to speak about their experiences in the television series, *The Vietnam War*, written by Geoffrey C. Ward and directed by Ken Burns and Lynn Novick.

The public heroes of people of color

Before turning to unsung heroes and heroines, it is useful to remember that the strikers and founders of ethnic studies clearly looked up to courageous people of color who were being recognized by the larger society, though not necessarily as heroes. These included Muhammad Ali (aka Cassius Clay) who refused to be drafted or to serve in the Vietnam War. He asked, "Why should they ask me to put on a uniform and go 10,000 miles from home and drop bombs and bullets on brown people in Vietnam while so-called Negro people in Louisville are treated like dogs and denied simple human rights?" One of his many famous quotes was, 'I ain't got no quarrel with them Viet Cong." At 25 years old, Muhammad Ali was stripped of his world boxing champion title. His boxing license was suspended.

Reverend Doctor Martin Luther King, Jr, the 1964 Nobel Peace Prize honoree and international hero for the Civil Rights Movement in the American rural South, courageously expanded his reach to the American urban North. He reached beyond civil rights to human rights and the fight against the Vietnam War. On April 4, 1968, at 39 years old, Dr. King was assassinated at Lorraine Motel in Memphis, TN, for daring to expand his vision from civil rights in the South to human rights around the world.

Perhaps the freshest heroes for the strikers and advocates for ethnic studies at San Francisco State were fellow students at San Jose State—the 1968 Summer Olympics gold medalist Tommie Smith and bronze medalist John Carlos, who bowed their heads and raised black gloved fists during the Olympics awards ceremony in Mexico City as it was broadcasted around the world. "The protest didn't stop with their fists. They also wore black socks and no shoes. On their clothes were badges of the Olympic Project for Human Rights, a group dedicated against racial segregation and racism in sports. Also, wearing the patch in support of Smith and Carlos was Australian 200-meter silver medalist Peter Norman."[9]

The Students

In my view, the students were and continue to be the most unsung heroes and heroines in the fight for ethnic studies. This observation is based on almost 50 years of reflection plus professional and volunteer work with a variety of students and interns during my Washington, DC-based federal career, as well as during retirement back in San Francisco.

In traditional and pre-industrial cultures, formal rites of passage signify the change from child to adult, from boy to man, from girl to woman. In the Latino tradition, the Quinceañera celebrates the coming of age of a girl from childhood to young womanhood on her fifteenth birthday and is one example. Post-industrial cultures by contrast have less formal rites. Popular movies such as the 2006 "Failure to Launch" depict persons over the legal adult age of 21 as being in arrested adolescence. When military service was mandatory from World War II through the Vietnam War, young men and women assumed adult responsibilities at eighteen years of age, or after high school graduation. By contrast, in the

---

9 Katie McLaughlin, "Eight Unforgettable Ways 1968 Made History," *CNN*, July 7, 2014, http://www.cnn.com/2014/07/31/us/1968-important-events/index.html.

twenty-first century, with the prevalence of post-graduate education, it is not uncommon for many persons over 21 years of age to have a primary status as students. For San Francisco State and other college students in the latter part of the twentieth century, entrance to and graduation from college served as the passage to adult responsibility.

The news clips and videotapes of San Francisco State College in 1968–1969 depict a student body largely dressed as members of the middle class; young adults ready to be in the white and blue collar work force. Many young women wear skirts and dresses with flats; several young men are in sports coats and jackets. At that point in history, college students were a privileged small group. In 1968, only 13.3 percent of men and 8 percent of women in the population had completed four or more years of college. National news clips show largely white student, faculty, and staff populations across American college campuses. Most college students of color were, or were aspiring to be, middle-class Americans. In *Agents of Change*, we see this view was embraced by the Cornell students much more than the San Francisco State students. For students and the American population, there were only 3 major television networks and no mobile phones or internet. The American population was limited to similar news and information. Furthermore, most Americans identified themselves as middle class or working class aspiring to the middle class.

According to then San Francisco State librarian and later strike archivist Helene Whitson, "At San Francisco State, I found well-dressed young men and women going about their academic activities. The student population appeared mostly white, although there were certainly students of color. . . . There were not that many courses or programs that addressed the specific needs of students of color . . . many students of color really wanted and needed specific information that they could learn and take back to their communities, in order to help the members of their various communities. They also felt that the histories of their various communities were being ignored. I think that students of color also felt that the administration and perhaps even some of the faculty members were dismissive of their issues and problems. They wanted to be heard, and many administrators did not take their needs seriously."[10]

San Francisco State was a largely commuter or "streetcar" college of about 18,000 students. It was a model institution for higher education in an urban setting with a pluralistic community. It had a national reputation for innovation and flexibility given programs like the Experimental College and the Tutorial Program. The Associated Students, Inc. had a sizable budget to run traditional campus activities as well as off campus programs such as tutorial programs in the inner city and work-study programs. It had a sizable number of students over 21 years of age and a portion who were married, employed full- or part-time, and even parents. As commuters, campus life was very pragmatic—take your classes; go to the bookstore; and study in the library. There were two dormitories, one for 400 young men and 400 for young women. There were married student housing apartments for less than a hundred graduate student couples. There was a lack of physical and social amenities with no Student Union—just huts for student organizations by the cafeteria. The professors shared crowded faculty offices and carried a 12-hour teaching load. In this very utilitarian and egalitarian environment, students and faculty displayed a live-and-let-live pragmatism.

"In the beginning of 1968, the student population of SF State was approximately 76% white, 9% Oriental/Filipino, 5% Black, 2% Mexican American, and 0.5% American Indian. A coalition of minority students merged and became known as the Third World Liberation Front (TWLF) to advocate for the needs of Third World students. The groups included the Asian American Political Alliance (AAPA), Black Student Union (BSU), Intercollegiate Chinese for Social Action (ICSA), the Latin American Student Organization (LASO), the Mexican American Student Confederation (MASC) and the Pilipino American Collegiate Endeavor (PACE). Among the most visible non-TWLF student organizations were the Students for a Democratic Society (SDS) and the Progressive Labor

---

10 "'On strike! Shut it down!' An Interview with Helene Whitson on the San Francisco College Strike and Strike Collection," interview by Anne Reynes, *E-rea* 10, no. 2 (2013), https://erea.revues.org/3182.

Party (PLP), both already active in the anti-war movement."[11] These students of color were motivated for college and raised by parents who believed that education was the way out of alien status and second class citizenship. They entered San Francisco State via the regular admissions process. Despite this reality, students on strike, especially students of color, were oftentimes depicted as unqualified students, agitators, and troublemakers by some politicians and larger community off campus. The media labeled them as militant and from the ghetto.

What is not often noted is that prior to November 6, 1969 and the years preceding the strike—before major coverage by outside media—attempts were made to meet the concerns of students of color. Faculty and administrators under the tenure of SF State presidents John Summerskill and Robert Smith attempted to resolve the prior demands for Black Studies and representation of minority students and faculty within campus. Initially, even Mayor Joseph Alioto commented on San Francisco's State pioneering approach to make college accessible to underrepresented groups. "This is a significantly new approach to the problem of education in the ghetto. . . . All credit for such a far sighted program should go to students, faculty, and administrators of the college. . . . This is like a new jobs program. . . . We're making the entrance examination subsequent to admission, rather than precedent."[12]

Through the earlier part of 1968, the BSU, the Third World student organizations, the Associated Students, Inc. and the Experimental College worked with faculty and administration. Their larger goals to end the war in Vietnam and address racism in the United States were manifested in specific demands for the college administration to end the Air Force ROTC on campus; to retain history professor Juan Martinez who was an adviser to Third World students; to admit 400 students of color under the college's ongoing special admissions program; and to hire minority faculty members. In protest of these unfilled demands, on

---

11   Jerry Dear, Katherine General, Susan Jeong, Lynne Wong, and Nancy Yin, "Asian Americans in the Third World Student Strike," *Dreams, Realities, and Challenges in Asian American Studies* (San Francisco: San Francisco State University, 1998), 9.

12   *San Francisco Chronicle*, May 2, 1968, Helene and William Whitson Scrapbook, SF State Library Strike Archives.

May 21, about 400 students held a nine-hour sit-in in the Administration building. Police were called to remove them. Student response was swift with protests on May 23 led by SDS and BSU/TWLF. The day after, John Summerskill was asked to resign his presidency by California State Colleges Chancellor Glenn Dumke. The students and community supporters from that protest and other events leading to the November 6, 1968 strike have not been as noted as much as those of fall 1968.

Several years earlier, Black students from the South, including Jerry Varnado and Jimmy Garrett, steeped in the experience of the largely working class and middle class Civil Rights Movement, came to San Francisco State for undergraduate and graduate school. They joined the on-campus Negro Students Association. By 1966, Varnado, Garrett, and Mariana Waddy were instrumental in replacing the Negro Student Association with the Black Student Union. This was consistent with the national shift from a mainstream-imposed term, "Negro," to the self-determination embodied by Black Power and "Black Is Beautiful." It was the first BSU in the nation, with other BSUs forming on other college campuses shortly thereafter. As young adults and the future leaders of their community, the San Francisco State BSU understood the importance of college access for young Black students to improve their life conditions. They collaborated for broader admissions criteria to enroll Black students through non-traditional means, such as the special admissions that existed for athletes or for legacy admissions that were open to children of alumni. Other programs were added, such as tutoring in San Francisco neighborhood schools, providing services to Black neighborhoods, developing Black Studies courses, hiring Black faculty, and providing supportive services to special admissions students or nontraditional students. These programs served not just Black people but other people as well—students of color, low-income and rural students not represented in the traditional student population. By 1968, similar initiatives were being articulated by the other student organizations of color that went on to unite their numbers and power as the Third World Liberation Front.

The presence of police, especially the Tactical Squad, on campus was contentious and discouraged by Summerskill and Smith, even though on November 13, 1968, police in full riot gear arrested students and others. As captured on video in November 1968, viewers can see White, Black, and Asian students mingle together on campus and watch the SFPD get in formation. Students and faculty members offer comments on Chancellor Dumke's decision to override college administration and whether police presence on campus quells or escalates violence. Canuto "Sonny" Aranaydo, a Filipino/American Indian student, observes that the strike was going well and peaceably before police presence. A White student notes that he saw a plainclothes officer in a departmental office. One Black student comments that Governor Reagan should remove the Tactical Squad from campus as they are not carrying student body identification cards.[13]

By contrast, the successor of Summerskill and Smith, S.I. Hayakawa, was named acting president on November 26th and welcomed the law enforcement officers. On December 3, known as "Bloody Tuesday," not only were students the target of police action, but according to Jason Ferreira and others, faculty, campus staff, medics, photographers, prominent Black leaders, and even church officials were indiscriminately beaten.[14] As police presence escalated on campus with violence against students and others, including bystanders, the student body became sympathetic to the strikers and their demands. Just as major newspapers and networks captured law enforcement brutality and violence towards the members of the Civil Rights Movement and Anti-Vietnam War Movement in prior years, they also recorded armed police beating unarmed folks at San Francisco in 1968–1969. Cameras also documented the circling of several helicopters above campus for surveillance and who-knew-what else along with the Tactical Squad and police mounted on horses.

From today's vantage point, what is clear is that the San Francisco State strike was not an isolated event or an outlier. It was one large data point—a significant milestone—among the acts of resistance on college

---

13 "San Francisco State faculty & student views," *The SF State College Strike Collection*, https://diva.sfsu.edu/collections/sfbatv/bundles/187202.
14 Jason Ferreira as quoted by Tanya Schevitz in "Remembering the Turbulent Time," *San Francisco Chronicle*, October 26, 2008.

campuses locally and globally against the war in Southeast Asia and the institutional subordination and segregation of peoples of color. It stands out and is remembered uniquely because a numerical minority of working class and middle-income students of color were leading the resistance, supported by a majority of white students and faculty, their families, communities, and off campus networks. Not only were they protesting the war, they were also warning of the deteriorating gap between the educational and employment opportunities for people of color compared to whites and the inequitable adherence to rule of law and due process that subjugated people of color. The role of individual students is detailed in Chapter 3, which highlights the youthfulness of the BSU/TWLF and College of Ethnic Studies leadership and those who followed them.

Practical Grassroots Activists

Margaret Leahy, one of the student activists prior to the Fall 1968–1969 BSU/TWLF strike, provides an eyewitness perspective and concise summary of the events before and during 1968 in her essay, "I was there," which appears in *On Strike! We're Gonna Shut it Down: The 1968–69 San Francisco State Strike*. Her description of "Bloody Tuesday" succinctly depicts how students, faculty, staff and the larger community quickly became practical grassroots activists.

> "All those who participated in the Strike know Tuesday, December 3, as "Bloody Tuesday." Joining about 2,500 student and faculty demonstrators at a noon rally were leaders of the Black, Asian, and Latino communities, as well as religious leaders. By the end of the rally, one non-striker estimated the crowd at approximately 5,000. The rally was attacked—no other word describes what occurred—by police coming from all sides. Fighting between police and demonstrators filled the central campus. The two sides were not evenly matched. While the demonstrators outnumbered the police, the police were armed with clubs and guns. Unarmed students lost all fear and jumped on the backs of police who were beating students, only to be pulled off and clubbed to the ground themselves.

The afternoon was bloody! Hayakawa, however characterized it as the most exciting day since his tenth birthday when he rode a roller coaster for the first time!

"There were 32 arrests and not only students were arrested. Carlton Goodlett, editor of The Sun-Reporter, a Black newspaper, was unceremoniously taken to jail and the Reverend Gerald Pederson, the campus minister of Ecumenical House, was arrested after being pushed to the ground with a club pressed against his clerical collar. In reaction to the police riot, support for the Strike swelled. Numerous community groups and religious leaders used their platforms to condemn the police, the City, and Hayakawa, which garnered even greater support for the Strike. The campus chapter of the American Federation of Teachers (AFT) began to pressure the San Francisco Central Labor Council for strike sanction. Even the Friends of the IRA came out in support of the Strike and publicly chastised their Irish brethren in the police forces for forgetting their own history of oppression and fighting for the wrong side."[15]

The Third World Liberation Front and the Members of the Select Committee

Another set of unlikely actors were the TWLF BSU representatives and the San Francisco State Members of the Select Committee, who were chosen to address the Fifteen Demands of the BSU and the TWLF and end the strike. By early 1969, after the massive arrests of hundreds of students, faculty, and community, emotional, social, legal, and financial costs were rising. The costs were great for individuals and for the campus. Many of the TWLF leaders were arrested and several served time in jail. Faculty and administrators were torn about supporting the student strike as well as the strike of the American Federation of

---

15 Margaret Leahy, "I was there…," *On Strike! We're Gonna Shut it Down: The 1968-69 San Francisco State Strike*, http://www.foundsf.org/index.php?title=On_Strike!_We%27re_Gonna_Shut_it_Down.

Teachers that supported the student strike but struck primarily for their own employment and academic freedom issues. Politicians and college administrators worried about shutting down all state college campuses in California. The subsequent Third World Liberation Front strike at UC Berkeley for an Ethnic Studies department was felt with even greater force. While San Francisco Mayor Joseph Alioto had ordered the SFPD Tactical Squad at SF State, at UC Berkeley, Governor Ronald Reagan called out the National Guard. Tear gas was used on strikers and protestors there. Campuses across the nation exploded. To their credit, the student and administration leaders at SF State understood that dragging out the strike in the spring 1969 semester with more external scrutiny and outside parties was not a healthy bargaining position. Thus, despite the losses noted above, the San Francisco State student-led strike ended peaceably, with faculty, administrators, student leaders, and community liaisons continuing to dialogue on and off campus. Hence, on March 19, 1969, the strike ended with review of and responses to the fifteen TWLF strike demands. Not all the demands were met—such as the hiring or retention of specific faculty but there was agreement on the larger issues of increasing numbers of traditionally underrepresented populations, specifically students of color from San Francisco and neighboring schools, and the creation of a School of Ethnic Studies. On March 20, Benny Stewart, as the representative of the BSU/TWLF Central Committee, recognized the support of revolutionary white students and noted that while institutional racism continued to exist, the strike settlement was a foundation for revolutionary change on campus and in communities. There exists a March 18, 1969 document titled, "Joint Agreement of the TWLF/BSU and the Members of the Select Committee Concerning Resolution of the Fifteen Demands and Other Issues Arising from the Student Strike at San Francisco State College, November 6, 1968 – March 18, 1969." The document names the Select Committee members as Curt Aller, Chairman, Select Committee, Donald Barnhart, Jordan Churchill, John Edwards, DeVere E. Pentony and Larry Robinson. Beneath these is a line, "APPROVED" and a following line reading S.I. Hayakawa, Acting President.[16] The SF State College Archives copies of this agreement do not show any signatures and the names of the Third World Liberation Front Representatives/Central Committee members are not even typed. Acting President Hayakawa states that he did not feel it was necessary for him to personally sign the Select committee agreement. While the representatives of the administration and TWLF Central Committee urged all student penalties be reduced to written reprimands, except for students who were convicted of violence, Acting President Hayakawa did not. He echoed Governor Ronald Reagan's comment that each case be treated individually.

The Faculty

During the 1968 -1969 student-led strike, Creative Writing professor Kay Boyle noted that faculty formed the Faculty Action Committee, whose aim was to protect students and to be a buffer between students and the San Francisco Police Tactical Squad.[17] In 1968, there were very few white women and people of color who were university professors, let alone tenured, not just at San Francisco State but across the nation. Many were still junior professors and raising young families. They were post World War II pioneers who entered academia, often as the first PhDs from their communities. They were not white males. In 1966, Black sociologist/psychologist Nathan Hare was recruited by then president John Summerskill to develop and lead the Black Studies Department. Mexican American historian Juan Martinez was hired to develop a program to bring more minority students on campus, including Mexican and Pilipino Americans. Black Panther minister George Murray was hired to teach general education English classes. What these faculty were attempting was new and innovative, even risky. They offered assertive support of greater representation of students and faculty of color on campus beyond and perhaps contrary to traditional Eurocentric criteria, including support of the TWLF BSU Fifteen Demands. Not so surprisingly, Hare,

---

16 "Joint Agreement," *The SF State College Strike Collection*, https://diva.sfsu.edu/collections/strike/bundles/ 187925.
17 "Introduction: Dissent by the Bay, Kay Boyle in San Francisco," *E-rea* 10, no. 2 (2013), https://erea.revues.org/3182.

Martinez and Murray were all dismissed, along with Summerskill and Robert Smith. Other striking faculty who were terminated included Bill Stanton, Bill Carpenter, and John "Tito" Gerassi.

Several white faculty also went on strike in support of the students even though the American Federation of Teachers (AFT) was primarily concerned with faculty labor issues in early 1969. Many held classes off campus for the safety of students. Among the white faculty who spoke up were Anatole Anton and Eric Solomon. A few were arrested. Bill Stanton of the AFT was the only full professor fired. Early on, Stanton pointed out SF State's failure to recruit minority students from the city of San Francisco.

For the new discipline of Ethnic Studies, "Recruiting faculty was a particularly challenging task. Some of the choices of courses offered that first semester were decided on the basis of who was available with appropriate expertise to teach on short notice."[18] Other faculty who already had appointments in traditional departments could have easily stayed in the comforts of the ivory tower but chose not to do so. One was Beatrice Medicine, an anthropologist and member of the Lakota Nation and of the Standing Rock Sioux Tribe. Professor Medicine was a trailblazer as an early American Indian woman with a PhD. She was faculty in the Anthropology Department and stepped up to the plate to serve as the first chair of Native American Studies (later named American Indian Studies). Throughout her career as a scholar-activist, she had a steadfast commitment to the self-determination of American Indians. Another was Kai-yu Hsu, who was a professor of Humanities and Foreign Languages. According to Marlon Hom, "The late Professor Kai-yu Hsu, an avid Strike supporter who quit as Chair of World Literature in protest against S.I. Hayakawa, held classes on campus. At noon, he would leave the picket sign behind the bushes, walk back to his office in the Psychology Building, and promptly begin his classes at 4:00 or 7:00."[19] Kai Yu Hsu also sent a memo to interested colleagues and

---

18   Malcolm Collier and Daniel Phil Gonzales, "Creation and Survival: Courses and Academic Programs, 1969-1986," *At 40: Asian American Studies @ San Francisco State* (San Francisco: Thomson-Shore Inc., 2009).

19   Marlon Hom, *Dreams, Realities, and Challenges in Asian American Studies*, 5.

students giving a chronological summary of the events leading up to the crisis.[20]

A story often recounted through the years by members of TWLF student organization Asian American Political Alliance (AAPA) at San Francisco State and by Jim Hirabayashi himself was that AAPA members saw his Japanese name on a faculty directory. He was only the second Asian American faculty at SF State when he was hired in 1959. Led by Penny Nakatsu and Masayo Suzuki, AAPA students knocked on his office door in the Anthropology Department and asked that he be their faculty sponsor; join the strike line; and be the adviser for the planning committee for the Asian American Studies curriculum for Chinese American, Pilipino, and Japanese American Studies. Professor Hirabayashi who, along with his family was interned during World War II, had just returned from a sabbatical covering the Biafra famine precipitated by the Nigerian civil war. According to his son, Lane, "So the strike had a HUGE impact on Jim. I know he credited the strike with turning his world around, and giving him a whole new vision and purpose." Lane also credits his dad with counseling his older brother, sociologist Gordon Hirabayashi, to appeal his World War II Supreme Court decision of curfew violation as a person of Japanese ancestry even though he was a citizen.[21] In 1987, the Court of Appeals for the Ninth Circuit granted a writ of coram nobis, overturning the conviction for which he had been imprisoned.

The courage and leadership of the Black faculty at San Francisco State before and after the strike and through the evolution of Black Studies have often been in the background to the BSU leaders and more well-known representatives of the Black community. In 1968, they were organized into the Black Faculty Union, perhaps some 15 in all. They were involved in the November 20, 1968 college convocation to bring together representatives of the college administration, faculty, and Third

20 "Memo Summarizing Chronology of Events, January 3, 1969," *The SF State College Strike Collection*, https://diva.sfsu.edu/collections/strike/bundles/187931.
21 Lane Hirabayashi, personal communication with author, October 29, 2017.

World Liberation Front to "discuss in a rational manner what is possible with regard to resolving the present crisis.[22] Two Black administrators, Dean of Student Activities Elmer Cooper and Dean of Undergraduate Studies Joseph White, joined the Third World students on stage. Cooper noted that the Trustees were worried about a Black Studies Department having an all-Black faculty yet they didn't mention that there were departments with all-white faculties. He named their fear of giving Black people control over their own destinies.[23] In an SFSC Black Faculty Press Release dated February 26, 1969, the Black Faculty Union called on Black educators in the Bay Area, the newly-formed Afro American Educators Association, independent professors, public school teachers, and other members of the Black middle class to acknowledge the SFSC was the birthplace of the Black Students Union (vanguard of the Black student movement). "As their professors and counselors, we the Black faculty, must begin to serve as a guiding force, giving a sense of direction, nationwide, to the Black educators' revolution."[24] At a press conference on June 29, 1969, Dr. White and Dean Cooper with two other senior Black faculty or administrators resigned from their posts. The latter were Edward Reavis, assistant dean of students, and Reginald Major, director, Educational Opportunity Program. Joseph White stated, "There is one and only one purpose to reducing EOP: to prevent non-white students from enrolling in this college ... Under these conditions, we can only submit our resignations."[25]

Another set of faculty yet to be fully recognized are several of the first professors of ethnic studies. A few had PhDs from elite universities, such as Nathan Hare in Black Studies from the University of Chicago and Jim Hirabayashi in Asian American Studies from Harvard University. At the same time, they held alternative, nontraditional perspectives and

---

22 William Barlow and Peter Shapiro, *An End to Silence: The San Francisco State Student Movement in the 60s* (New York: Pegasus, 1971), 239.
23 Ibid., 240.
24 Third World Liberation Front Folder, SF State Library Strike Archives, San Francisco State College.
25 "Faculty resignations at SF State," The SF State College Strike Collection, San Francisco State University, https://diva.sfsu.edu/collections/strike/bundles/187239.

experience due to their minority status.

Other pioneer ethnic studies faculty were not career professors. Some did not have graduate degrees. Philip Choy was an architect and president of the Chinese Historical Society of America when George Woo asked him and Him Mark Lai, who trained as a mechanical engineer, to teach the first Chinese American history class in Asian American Studies in 1969. In reflecting on 40 years of ethnic studies, Choy commented, "When Him Mark Lai and I entered the classroom, students involved in the Strike sized us up. Confident that the material to be presented justified the cause for the Strike, I was not intimidated. Him Mark Lai, being the scholar that he is, insured that the course met, if not surpassed, academic standards . . . Now forty years after the Strike at San Francisco State, we have validated our presence in America without yielding to Anglo American dominance. We have reclaimed our history, defined our own identity, shaped our own destiny. Now forty years later, we have a piece of America's apple pie, baked by our own bakers. I never dreamed I would witness these changes in my lifetime. Participation in the Movement, and teaching at San Francisco State, are milestones in my life."[26] One of the first Black Studies professors and a founding member of the Black Studies Department was Patricia Thorton, AKA Chinosole, who supported the SF State strike. She taught Black literature in the south after the end of segregation, edited *Schooling of the Generations in the Politics of Prison* (Afrikan/Black Prison Educational Fund, 1996), and authored *African Diaspora and Autobiographics: Skeins of Self and Skin* (Peter Lang Publishers, 2001). Chinosole was the chair of Women Studies at SF State from 1990–1992.

Jovina Navarro was a newly-minted PhD in Psychology when she was approached by PACE and the Asian American Studies Planning Group to create and teach the first Pilipino Community workshop. She was a scholar-activist who also worked with the senior service center in Chinatown Manilatown. She developed community fieldwork curriculum. She went on to be emeritus professor at San Jose State.

---

26 Philip P. Choy, "Upon Reflection," *At 40*, 79.

Staff

The role of staff during the strike is not well documented but, like the faculty, they stood between the police force and unarmed students to protect the latter on various occasions. One student-staff was Steve Zeltzer, an SDS member who worked in the library and was arrested several times. Roger Alvarado spoke of the bravery of cafeteria staff. More than once in fall 1968, police would go in search of individuals on campus grounds and inside buildings. Much of the mass demonstration and activities were around noon at the Free Speech Speakers Platform. The cafeteria was yards away. Students and others would disperse there as police appeared. The police would enter the cafeteria, pushing chairs and harassing folks even as they ate. As students went to hide in the cooking area, the cooks, cashiers, and bus people stood between the students and police.[27] College staff that supported the strike and lost jobs included janitors and those who worked in the Dining Hall, Faculty Room, and the Associated Students.

San Francisco State Strike Veterans

The symbol of SF State BSU/TWLF and College of Ethnic Studies is four fingers with a thumb closed in a fist signifying unity in brown, red, yellow, white and black colors with the words "Relevant Education." The veteran strikers—students, faculty/staff and community—represented the population of San Francisco and California. This reality of pluralism—*e pluribus unum*—from many, one, is not gleaned from the mainstream print and audio visual media of 1968–1969, nor in many of the early books during and immediately following the end of the strike and the establishment of ethnic studies. It comes from documents created by the San Francisco State Strike veterans and those who followed them. One such document is the commemoration booklet, "The People, the Soul of the Strike: A Work in Progress," created by the Archive Committee of the 40th Anniversary of the 1968 SF State Black Student Union/Third World Liberation Front student-led Strike. This

---

27   Jonathan Craig, *Activist State: A Documentary About The 1968 San Francisco Student Strike*, 2009 YouTube Video, 26:16, posted by "Jonathan Craig," February 10, 2013, https://www.youtube.com/watch?v=aoPmb-9ctGc.

booklet featured the strike and ethnic studies student leaders, as well as faculty, staff and administration in their own words. It is a brief but powerful testimony because it confirms the wide range of San Francisco State students, faculty and staff instrumental in the strike and ethnic studies, made up of people of color and whites. The veterans speak for themselves on their role in the strike, what resonated for them at the commemoration, and their personal sacrifices. Many were appreciative of the experience of solidarity and community, seeing their decision to honor the strike and establish ethnic studies as a transformative privilege. This experience guided the rest of their lives, despite personal and collective sacrifices. In the extensive videos of that commemoration, participants are glad to see each other and reunite after forty years. There is an ease in how their stories complement each other, with many laughs and smiles. There is a satisfying camaraderie of veterans, of brotherhood and sisterhood. It thoughtfully captures students, faculty and staff, and colleagues in memoriam.

In his seminal dissertation, Jason Ferreira writes, "In San Francisco, Asian, Black, Latina, and Native American women actively contributed to the struggles to reclaim Alcatraz, defend Los Siete, and establish an Ethnic Studies program; yet, they often had to simultaneously fight to define "liberation" and "self-determination" in non-masculinist terms. The militarism, for example, so prevalent within various radical organizations, at times reflected an entrenched machismo and a reactionary conception of power."[28] Just as in the Civil Rights Movement and anti-war movement, where men were the public leaders and the role of women as leaders was overshadowed, the unsung heroines of San Francisco State were pivotal to the student-led strike and the creation and maintenance of ethnic studies. By the time of the 40th anniversary of the 1968 SF State Black Student Union/Third World Liberation Front Student-led Strike, the role of women was center stage. In addition to the commitment and experiences articulated in, "The People, The Soul of the Strike: A Work in Progress," the "Welcome to the Commemoration"

---

28 Jason Michael Ferreira, "All Power to the People: A Comparative History of Third World Radicalism in San Francisco, 1969-1974," PhD diss., (University of California, Berkeley, 2003), 24.

letter was co-signed by Kenneth P. Monteiro, Dean, College of Ethnic Studies and Ginger Yamamoto, Director, Educational Opportunity Program. The panel, "Women in the Strike: Then and Now," presented the pivotal roles of women of color and white women.[29] While individual young women are portrayed in Chapter 3, SF State Emeritus Collections Librarian Helene Whitson is noted here for her fastidious collection of various items during the strike of her own volition. She compiled the SF Strike collection that resides in the university Archives. The Helene and William Whitson Scrapbook, *Crisis at San Francisco State College: 1967-1969* resides in the Special Collections of the J. Paul Leonard Library at SF State. It includes a chronological index and contains newspaper clippings and articles related to the SF State strike. Additionally, Helene Whitson continued to collect strike materials from faculty groups, student groups, off campus participants, as well as members of the library staff and faculty.[30] Sharon Gold Martinas also provided her collection to the San Francisco State Strike Archives. This is a diverse collection of materials from a wide range of strike participants including copies of "Black Fire," the BSU newsletter, and the various position papers of TWLF organizations by the Black Students Union, Philippine Collegiate Endeavor, Mexican American Student Confederation, and Intercollegiate Chinese for Social Action.

Those Arrested, Those Prosecuted
William Barlow and Peter Shapiro dedicated their book, *An End to Silence: The San Francisco State Student Movement in the 60s* to the S.F. State 700, "all of whom were arrested and prosecuted for their participation in the student strike." Some individuals were arrested more than once,

29 "Women in the Strike, Then and Now," The SF State College Strike Collection, https://diva.sfsu.edu/collections/ coes/bundles/218251, and "The People, the Soul of the Strike: A Work in Progress," pictorial booklet prepared for the commemoration of the 40th Anniversary of the 1968 SF State Black Student Union (BSU)/Third World Liberation Front (TWLF) Student Led Strike, San Francisco State.
30 "San Francisco State University Strike Scrapbook - April 7, 1969," The SF State College Strike Collection, https://diva.sfsu.edu/collections/strike/bundles/187428.

including BSU/ TWLF leaders Bridges Randall, Jerry Varnado, Roger Alvarado, and Hari Dillon and SDS leader Todd Gitlin. Several were professors including Nathan Hare, Fred Thalheimer (Sociology), William Carpenter (International Relations) and Anatole Anton (Philosophy). The first huge number of arrests was on January 6, 1969, "The San Francisco Chronicle noted that on one day alone, January 23, 1969, 454 persons were arrested for violating S.I. Hayakawa's edict limiting campus assembly. The majority of those arrested were young white males; 187 were women, 33 to 42 were persons over the age of thirty; 30 were Blacks and 26 Orientals. Based on a review of addresses, 23 Bay Area communities were involved."[31]

Those arrested over the strike period were primarily charged with unlawful assembly, refusal to disperse, and/or disturbing the peace. Several arrested students, led by Carmen Carrillo, asked that these laws be declared unconstitutional in that they allegedly violated free speech and assembly guarantees. A panel of three federal judges declined to do so.[32] Through the rest of 1969 trials were held. In August, 19 trials were held (sometimes by groups rather than individually), with 79 persons found guilty, 50 acquitted and 6 deadlocked.[33] George Colbert, Edward de la Cruz and Kathleen Ennis were sentenced to 120 days with 90 days suspended and 3 years of probation. Laureen Chew spent one month at trial, a year on appeal and twenty days in jail.[34]

Parents, Community Organizations, and Others

The role of parents, community organizations, and others in the SF State strike and creation of ethnic studies was crucial but not well-publicized

---

31 "White Majority in State Arrests," *San Francisco Chronicle*, January 25, 1969 in *San Francisco Examiner*, SF State Strike, 1968-1969, box 2, San Francisco History Center/San Francisco Public Library.
32 "San Francisco State Arrests Constitutional," *San Francisco Examiner*, June 29, 1969 in *San Francisco Examiner*, SF State Strike, 1968-1969, box 2, San Francisco History Center/San Francisco Public Library.
33 "SF State Jury Still Out," *San Francisco Examiner*, August 20, 1969 in *San Francisco Examiner*, SF State Strike, 1968-1969, box 2, San Francisco History Center/San Francisco Public Library.
34 Laureen Chew, "A Journey to 20 Days in the Hole," *At 40*, 24.

initially. In Abby Ginzburg and Frank Dawson's 2016 documentary *Agents of Change*, a pivotal moment of visual support for the striking students is when parents, neighbors, community organizations, government officials, and religious leaders come on campus and voice support for the TWLF BSU 15 Demands and speak against the violence inflicted on strikers and supporters. On December 2, 1968, 600 members of SFPD's Tactical Squad, mounted police, and California Highway Patrol staged a premeditated attack on about 2,000 persons on the strike picket line at a noon rally, which included civic leaders Ron Dellums, Willie Brown, Dr. Carlton Goodlett, and Rev. Cecil Williams. Estimates of arrested persons varied from 30 to 40. Appalled parents and community members responded quickly. On December 4th, led by Black parents and representatives from the National Urban League, Congress of Racial Equality, and the Western Addition Community Organization, among others, they met with President Hayakawa to recommend that he remove the police; suspend classes; and implement the BSU/TWLF fifteen demands. He did not. The parents and leaders of community organizations serving people of color continued to support the student demands throughout the strike. Some were arrested and jailed along with students and faculty.

Our parents were also very involved in the establishment of ethnic studies. For example, in Pilipino Studies/Asian American Studies, the community advisory board included chairman Julita Tamondong McLeod, who became the first Filipino American elementary school principal in the San Francisco Unified School District. Before joining the public school system, she had taught some of the strikers as fourth or fifth graders at Morning Star School in Japantown. Carolina Borromeo, a mother of twelve children, developed the first Introductory Pilipino History Class in fall 1969, commuting across town from the old Lowell High School during her lunch hour. Philippine Consul General Samson Sabalones provided resources, contacts, and use of the Philippine Consulate for meetings with the Pilipino Studies Planning Group, Pilipino Studies Community Advisory Board, and Filipino American business and professional associations. The home of my parents, Lazaro Tamayo and Anicia Lucas, was the site of many curriculum-planning meetings in 1969–1970. The other ethnic studies departments also had strong parental support, not just during the strike but in the establishment of the pioneer departments. Over the decades, the parents of students of COES contributed to, and continue to contribute to, scholarships and community and education projects.

Over the years, information about parental and community participation has become part of the San Francisco State University Strike Archives. In particular, the Sharon Martinas Collection contains ephemera such as an announcement titled, "Strike Support Rally, February 2, 1969 at the San Francisco Labor Temple, 2940 – 16th Street." A variety of speakers included Dr. Carlton Goodlett, publisher of the *The Sun Reporter*, Lou Goldblatt, Secretary/Treasurer, International Longshore and Warehouse Union/ILWU, Larry Itliong, Assistant Director, United Farm Workers/UFW, AFL-CIO, Rev. Lloyd K. Wake, Japanese American Strike Supporters, Salvador Cordova, Mission Strike Support, Ron Dellums, Berkeley City Council, and Ed Barlow, Secretary Treasurer, Teamsters Local 19. This event is also captured in the SF State College Strike Collection, San Francisco Bay Area Television Archive highlighting Dr. Goodlett's explanation of how local community and labor forces were mobilizing in unison to support student protests at SF State College, in anticipation of a protracted struggle to restructure California Higher Education system.[35] Another ephemera is titled, "Community Conference to Support the S.F. State" in *Community Conference Strike Bulletin*, vol. 1, no 2, February 27, 1969. This document notes a community meeting at Glide Memorial Church and a march by the Community Conference and Parents Support Committee via car and bus caravan to the Senate Education Committee hearing on the strike in Sacramento.

Along with Ben Williams, Belva Davis was one of only two Black, nonwhite mainstream reporters at the time. Belva's work began with

---

35 "Dr. Carlton Goodlett Press Conference," *The SF State College Strike Collection*, https://diva.sfsu.edu/collections/ strike/bundles/187252; Shane Murphy, *STRIKE: A Voice in Time – The SFSU Strikes of 1968*, 2015 YouTube video, 11:54, posted by "Shane Murphy," May 6, 2015, https://www. youtube.com/ watch?v=PiYYyHFHtnY.

the Black media including *The Sun-Reporter* and radio station KDIA AM, Boss Soul Radio in Oakland. As she began work with KPIX and then KQED, the advice she was given transitioning from a segregated to a mainstream audience was that she be a reporter for all the people now. Like Jim Vance and other Black media pioneers, she reported objectively on historic moments. She reported on campus during the strike, oftentimes in volatile situations. Her goal was to get the film to television stations and on the air as soon as possible.[36] Ms. Davis' long-term contribution to the strike and ethnic studies, along with KRON political editor Rollin Post, was ensuring that the 16 millimeter tapes of this period were salvaged and stored for years until they could properly be archived at San Francisco State.

The Martinas Collection includes the Lawrence Hyink Family Collection. Hyink was a white freshman in fall 1968. His mother, Mrs. Jordy Hyink, wrote a letter to Dr. Hayakawa and Mayor Alioto that she shared with the *San Francisco Examiner* and *San Francisco Chronicle* in a letter dated December 6, 1968. Mrs. Hyink raised several questions precipitated by the strike including: "Is there a conspiracy to destroy the State College system in California? Why was the controversy regarding Murray aggravated just before a general election in which the public would be voting on college bond issues? Why are college budgets being cut at a time when more students desire to enter college? Is it not more expensive to the taxpayer to suppress rational demands of the minority by force than to consider them and act on them?" While the files do not include a response to Mrs. Hyink's letter, there is a January 17, 1979 letter from Michael McCone, appointment Secretary to Mayor Joseph Alioto, to Lawrence Hyink turning down his request for an appointment with the mayor and the Parents Strike Support Committee.[37]

Various labor unions supported the student and faculty strikes, including the United Farmworker Association, which was comprised mainly of Filipino and Mexican workers. Larry Itliong spoke to the importance of the strike. Some of the first special admissions students were Latino and Filipino rural children, the first in their families to attend

---

36 Belva Davis, personal interview with author, January 29, 2018.
37 Hyink Family Archives, SFSU Archives 2015:08, box 1.

college. The American Federation of Teachers, the San Francisco Labor Council and the International Longshore and Warehouse Union (ILWU) endorsed the strike

An Ad Hoc Committee, Citizens Concerned for San Francisco State College wrote, "We believe that if the college is to achieve the greatest possible educational benefits to the community, it must fit itself to serve the felt needs of all ethnic groups. It has so far failed to do so for Black, brown and yellow students. And that failure is the more critical because minority groups, to a far greater degree than white students, must look to the State College as the main educational resource in working toward a bachelor's degree." It was signed by then San Francisco Supervisor Jack Morrison, Canon James B. Guinan, Diocese of California, Reverend John Chester Smith, San Francisco, Reverend William Grace of the United Presbyterian Church, John F. Delany, Executive Secretary of the Catholic Archdiocese, Committee on Social Justice, and Rita R. Semel, Coordinator, San Francisco Conference for Religion, Race and Social Concerns.[38]

Some religious communities also stepped up to support not the student strike per se but the student strike issues of self-determination and representation. On campus, the Ecumenical House United Campus Ministry included the Roman Catholic Newman Club and the California Med Campus Ministry. In early 1968, Ecumenical House released a statement, "We see campus ministry as one of the pilings of this bridge between campus and community. Like Hull House so Ecumenical House is a community center, but unlike Hull House, we are a place from which people go into the community, not a place for people to come to. We serve as a broker between various communities and the college."[39] A policy statement concerned with the use of Ecumenical House further stated, "The church has historically affirmed the freedom of conscience, protest, dissent and advocacy, and, in this instance, wishes to affirm this

38 "Ad Hoc Committee of Citizens Concerned for San Francisco State College," in San Francisco State University Strike Collection, Sharon Martinas Collection, box 10, folder 95, item 6.
39 "Abstract of United Campus Christian Ministry, January 3, 1968" in San Francisco State University Strike Collection, Sharon Martina Collection, box 10, item 95.

tradition." The leadership of Ecumenical House included Reverend John Jones, Reverend Dr. Gerald Pederson, Mr. Hannibal Williams and Mrs. Sarah Wylie. Located directly across campus on the northeast corner of Nineteenth Avenue and Holloway Avenue, Ecumenical House promoted an open door policy for students, faculty and staff, offering safe haven for meetings on campus disputes and a medical treatment center for persons injured in demonstrations. It also served as a gathering point before and after rallies.[40]

Off campus, individual parishes supported the student community programs. For example, under Father Eugene Boyle, Sacred Heart Church in the Fillmore in San Francisco was the site of BSU tutoring programs as well as the Black Panther breakfast program. The latter first began in January 1969 with Father Earl A. Neil at St. Augustine Church in West Oakland. The most visible support off campus came from the Black and multicultural congregations such as Reverend Cecil Williams, Reverend Lloyd Wake and Reverend Antonio Ubalde of Glide Methodist Church in the Tenderloin. Chinatown ministers also supported the strikers including Reverend Larry Jack Wong and Reverend Harry Chuck. Seminarians of St. Patrick's Seminary in Menlo Park, students of Father Boyle, produced a local version of the Kerner Commission report, the analysis of racial tensions that was written in the wake of the 1967 summer riots. The resulting 577-page "Little Kerner Report" concluded that white San Franciscans were "sleeping through a revolution."[41] Mayor Joseph Alioto condemned the report calling it, "…the product of 21-year-old students who have been secluded in their seminary and not in contact with the objective facts."[42] Campus newspapers along with San Francisco and national media provided daily coverage of the longest student-led strike in history. One documentary stands out, published by Labor Video in

---

40 Dr. Pedersen Interview, The SF State College Strike Collection, https://diva.sfsu.edu/collections/coes/bundles/ 218206.
41 Clint Reilly et al, "Little Kerner Report: San Francisco: A City in Crisis," *A Report to the Churches and Synagogues*, sponsored by the San Francisco Conference on Religion, Race and Social Concerns, April 1968.
42 Jeffrey M. Burns, "Eugene Boyle, the Black Panther Party and the New Clerical Activism" in *US Catholic Historian* (Vol 13. No. 3, Summer 1995), 147, http://www.jstor.org/stable25254518.

2014, which provides various points of view and depicts the widespread, diverse support of the strike. While *"The Turning Point," San Francisco State '68 Strike* condenses this period, it makes viewers not just think of but deeply feel the strike experience.[43]

Given 2018's focus on police violence against people of color, especially Black males, it is worth noting that one police organization deplored the police brutality of students at SF State in 1968–69. Black officer-led organization "The Officers for Justice" was composed of San Francisco Police Department Black and white officers and was formed in October 1968. In a statement signed "Keep the Faith," the group stated, "The Officers for Justice deplore the present use of Black police at San Francisco State College. If assigned to duty at San Francisco State College we will not tolerate misconduct on the part of our fellow officers."[44] Officers included Henry Williams, Palmer Jackson, Leroy Appleby, Hans Anderson, Obrie Boyd and Richard Hongisto.

The Planning Groups

Before the strike was even over, faculty, staff and students began to address the practical aspects of establishing the School of Ethnic Studies. At that point, work gradually shifted from the BSU/TWLF Central Committee to an Ethnic Studies Planning Group. Several of us, mainly undergraduate students, were fortunate enough to have participated in the strike and then be part of the planning groups. With the spring 1969 semester ending and summer approaching, many upper classmen and graduate student strike leaders had graduated, transferred, been deported, and/or been jailed. While initially staffed by students with several community advisors, the lead in the planning groups was then Dean of Academic Planning Daniel D. Feder, with support from Professor Jim Hirabayashi. Prior to coming to San Francisco State, Dan Feder had served as dean of students at the University of Denver and had a history of improving services for college students. He was past

---

43   Labor Video Project, "'The Turning Point' The San Francisco State '68 Strike," 2015 YouTube Video, 56:01, posted by "laborvideo," December 8, 2014, https://www.youtube.com/watch?v=Qd6-P3kHRBY.

44   "Police Slap at Cop Brutality," *The Daily Gater*, San Francisco State College, volume 100, number 64, January 16, 1969.

president of the American College Personnel Association (ACPA). Due to his leadership, ACPA was one of the first national organizations after World War II to adopt resolutions against holding professional meetings in any city that practiced discrimination.[45] Another key planning group participant was Carmen Carrillo. A Psychology graduate student and La Raza Studies representative, Carillo inspired the undergraduates by her example of never hesitating to ask difficult questions. Dean Feder "ran training workshops on administrative procedures, staffing formulas, the political aspects of the state legislative budgetary process, and important details of the administrative practice at the highest level of the college.[46] Dubbed by Daniel Gonzales "The Feder Seminars," Dean Feder ran the sessions like graduate seminars. He shared and explained the college's organizational charts and answered questions like "What is FTE?" and "What is the Academic Master Plan and how did it come about?"[47] From this general planning group, various departments developed more specific ones. Asian American Studies had a General Planning Group composed of the Chinese American Planning Group, the Japanese American Planning Group and the Pilipino American Planning Group. Early on, the group chose a consensus-based decision-making process. As Collier and Gonzales noted, "The difficulties of getting our program curriculum accepted by the broader institution as a whole should not be underestimated."

There were two overriding issues—creating a new discipline while adhering to SF State's departmental and curriculum processes. "When the strike ended in March of 1969 there was no Asian American Studies program anywhere, no models, no existing courses, no real body of curriculum to draw on, almost no books in print for courses or reference, and no body of trained and experienced specialists who could teach the

---

45 "Daniel Feder (1945 -1947)," *ACPA*, http://www.myacpa.org/daniel-d-feder.
46 Malcolm Collier and Daniel Gonzales, "Governance in AAS: Principles, Structure and Practice," *At 40*, 54.
47 "Feder Seminar: Notes on Economics of the College," Sharon Martinas Collection, box 6, folder 79.

course—nothing. We had to invent Asian American Studies."[48] With respect to processes, "The negotiated Strike settlement provided for the nominal establishment of Asian American Studies and the other programs in Ethnic Studies but each individual course proposed by any of our programs was required to be approved through the 'regular' channels via committees… then by the higher campus administration."[49] Throughout the spring and summer, students, faculty and community experts offered their services voluntarily on and off campus to ensure that by Fall 1969, students could register and attend courses in each of the Ethnic Studies departments. In addition, the importance of allowing Asian American Studies/Ethnic Studies courses to fulfill General Studies requirements was championed by George Woo and others. This strategic, some say brilliant, move facilitated a larger enrollment of not just students of color but all students from the start. This was an innovation of openness and inclusion so Asian American Studies and Ethnics Studies at SF State did not become specialized or ghettoized courses in search of students, faculty and staff. Instead, the program reached and served thousands of students through five decades.

Irene Dea joined what eventually became the Chinese American Planning group and remained so through 1977. After that she was worked the main AAS office, both for the Nine Unit Block and on general department issues. In 1976–77 she worked on The Association of Chinese Teachers' curriculum project, writing Chinese American history material for elementary schools, then later became long-time director of Wah Mei Bilingual Preschool and Childcare Center, and finally a teacher in SFUSD after 1986.[50]

Rosalie Alfonso reminded me that, like Daniel Feder, several administrators were crucial for the actual nuts and bolts of housing and stabilizing the new School of Ethnic Studies in the early 1970s. These include Provost Donald Garrity, Provost Lawrence Ianni, Lana

---

48   Malcolm Collier and Daniel Phil Gonzales, "Creation and Survival: Courses and Academic Programs, 1969-1986," *At 40*, 63.

49   Ibid., 64.

50   Malcolm Collier, personal communication with author, November 20, 2017.

Thomson of the Academic Senate, Registrar Laura Ware, Allen Willard of Academic Resources, and Sergio Torres, who was instrumental in the various interim office moves.[51]

The Institutional Memory of the College of Ethnic Studies

The last, but certainly not least, set of unsung heroes and heroines are the individuals who together constitute the institutional memory of the College of Ethnic Studies. While the 1968–69 student-led strike has a bounty of print and digital archives that provides institutional memory, such an archive is an evolving project for the College of Ethnic Studies. A major reason for the unbroken and long history of Ethnic Studies at San Francisco State is the institutional memory provided by individuals who went from being striking students to serving on the planning committee to developing and teaching community-relevant courses to maintaining the administrative structure of the college. At the 30th anniversary commemoration of Asian American Studies at San Francisco State, what was notable is that several faculty and administrative staff in October 1998 were students during the strike. Danilo Begonia and Jeffrey Paul Chan had been graduate students. Subsequently, Begonia served as acting dean of the college while Chan was chair of Asian American Studies. 1968 undergraduate Laureen Chew became associate dean of the College of Ethic Studies and faculty of the College of Education. Alfred Wong, who was chairman of the TWLF Central committee in 1969, was associate director of the college's Upward Bound Program in the 1970s.[52] From the 40th anniversary commemoration of the founding of the College of Ethnic Studies and approaching its 50th anniversary, Bette Matsuoka maintained due diligence on the college's finances. Similarly, Ellie Luis handled personnel issues for several years with a dedicated thoroughness and compassion. Dorothy (Dottie) Ross handled front office reception. As an undergraduate, Betty Inouye Matsuoka was captured in the news as a kimono-clad striker, along with Jane Tabata and Miyo Ohta. In the 40th anniversary commemoration book, "We the People, the Soul

---

51 Rosalie Alfonso, personal communication with author, June 14, 2018.
52 *Dreams, Realities, and Challenges in Asian American Studies*, (San Francisco: San Francisco State University, 1998).

Booklet," Betty noted, "I wasn't a major role player during the Strike and my parents didn't know I was part of the movement until my picture (showing me with an anti-Hayakawa picket sign) appeared on the front page of a San Francisco newspaper. My mother gave me two choices: I was to remove myself from this anarchy or I was on my own. I chose the latter."[53]

1969 striker and planning committee member Daniel P. Gonzales is the longest serving COES faculty member. He has mentored hundreds of students and served on various academic and community programs through the decades. He and Malcolm Collier have served as institutional memory of the college since its inception. Dan's tenure is topped only by Rosalie Alfonso, who has served as assistant to the COES Dean from 1971 through 2018. The fact that there have been only seven deans in almost 50 years is a testament to the quiet but sustained commitment of COES leaders for stability, continuity and growth despite challenges.

The Deans

For almost fifty years, one of the stabilizing influences of the College of Ethnic Studies is the long tenure of deans. For five decades, there have been seven: James A. Hirabayashi, 1969–1977 & 1979–1980, Danilo T. Begonia, 1978–1979, D. Phillip McGee, 1980–1999, Gerald West, 1999–2001, Tomas Almaguer, 2001–2004, Kenneth Monteiro, 2006–2018, and Amy Sueyoshi, interim, 2018.

---

53 *The People, the Soul of the Strike: A Work in Progress,* 14.

GOLDEN CHILDREN

CHAPTER 3

And the Children Shall Lead Us

Children and youth remind us that the status quo must make way for them. They tell their elders to move on. They lead as a new generation. The adults in their lives, however, sometimes send them to lead by putting them at the front lines in battle. Notwithstanding the lessons of the Vietnam War, which officially ended in 1975, the United States has continued to send its youth to fight undeclared wars in the Third World since March 2003 with no end in sight. The difference in the twenty-first century is that now the nation sends not just our sons but also our daughters to war.

Children and Youth First

Of the veterans of World War II, Christopher Nolan in his film *Dunkirk* noted, "One of the most striking things when you spoke to veterans of this conflict is they were just children when they went over there."[1] Similarly, in his 2017 documentary series on the Vietnam War, Ken Burns reminds us that this war was fought by children on both sides. The end of the Vietnam War is also attributed in large part to the young. Among the most visible segments of the population involved in the years-long active anti-war movement were youth, specifically college students in the US and abroad.

Nations identify their cream of the crop, "the brightest of the brightest," in various ways. In the US, a popular one is the Center for Talented Youth at Johns Hopkins University, which identifies academic talent from second grade through eighth grade. In the seventh grade, selected students from across the United States are invited to take the SAT (originally the Scholastic Aptitude Test). International students are also identified. These youth are further nurtured and tracked for academic success throughout their education, including college and graduate school. They represent a pool of talent and leadership for the

---

1 Eliza Berman, "Christopher Nolan's Great War," *Time*, July 31, 2017.

nation in both civilian and military careers.

A fictionalized version of this process was the military science fiction series, *Ender's Game*, by Orson Scott Card. The first novel in 1985, *Ender's Game*, introduced the boy protagonist, Andrew "Ender" Wiggin. As a very young child, he and similar children are identified as highly intelligent and gifted, taken away from their families and sent to military academy. Set in Earth's future, the novel presents humankind gearing up for a deadlier assault after two conflicts with the "buggers," an insectoid alien species. In preparation for an anticipated third invasion, Ender and his classmates are put through increasingly difficult games and tests to prepare to fight the enemy.

Just as youth formed the front lines of battle in wars among nations, they were at the forefront of the Civil Rights Movement to fight white supremacy or apartheid. In September 1957, The Little Rock Nine were fifteen and sixteen year-olds chosen to integrate Central High School. They faced opposition from Governor Orval Faubus, who deployed the Arkansas National Guard to block their entry. President Dwight Eisenhower ordered the 101st Airborne Division of the US Army to Little Rock and federalized the entire Arkansas National Guard. When the Little Rock Nine were admitted to Little Rock Central High, they withstood daily hostility and a year of physical and verbal abuse, including being spat on. One of the nine was Melba Pattillo Beals, who wrote a book published in 1994 titled, *Warriors Don't Cry: A Searing Memoir of the Battle to Integrate Little Rock's Central High*. In it she describes how one of the white students threw acid in her eyes. Governor Faubus shut down Little Rock's high schools the following school year. Melba moved to Santa Rosa, CA to finish high school. She attended and graduated from San Francisco State. There was also another teenage girl who was not always recognized as a heroine of the Civil Rights Movement. On March 2, 1955, 15-year-old Claudette Colvin was arrested in Montgomery, AL for refusing to give her seat to a white passenger. This was several months before 42-year-old Rosa Parks' more famous refusal on December 1, 1955.

The Freedom Riders were also teenagers, as noted by Michael Tubbs, the mayor of Stockton, CA, who was elected at 26 years old in 2016. In his biography, *True Son: A Documentary Film*, Mayor Tubbs mentions speaking to one of the original Freedom Riders, Bob Singleton, who asked him why August 4, 1961 was important. Tubbs responds because that was when Singleton was arrested as a 19-year-old Freedom Rider. Singleton responds that that was when Barack Obama was born, connecting his action from the past as precedent to the future election of the first Black American president. Singleton goes on to say that, in turn, Tubbs, as a civic leader today, will affect a young person 50 years from now.[2]

Another icon is Congressman John Lewis, one of the 13 original Freedom Riders and chairman of SNCC (Student Nonviolent Coordinating Committee) from 1963 to 1966. Representative Lewis was captured on national television as a 25-year-old, leading 600 marchers with Hosea William across the Edmund Pettus Bridge in Selma, Alabama. He was beaten by state troopers with nightsticks, leaving him bleeding and with his skull fractured. Black youth in the south were joined by counterparts from the north and west who were active in the Southern Freedom Movement of the 1960s. They were staff and volunteers for SNCC (Student Nonviolent Coordinating Committee), CORE (Congress of Racial Equality), SCLC (Southern Christian Leadership conference) and NAACP (National Association for the Advancement of Colored People), among others. As noted by historian Howard Zinn, "What the civil rights movement proved is that even if people lack the customary attributes of power—money, political authority, physical force—as did the Black people of the Deep South, there is a power that can be created out of pent-up indignation, courage, and the inspiration of a common cause, they can win . . . the reward for participating in a movement for social justice is not the prospect of future victory. It is the exhilaration of standing together with other people, taking risks together, enjoying small triumphs and enduring disheartening setbacks—together."[3] When today's popular media views coming of age at the beginning of the

---

2 *True Son*, DVD, directed by Kevin Gordon (2014; True Son, 2014).
3 Howard Zinn, *You Can't Be Neutral on a Moving Train: A Personal History of Our Times* (Boston: Beacon Press, 1994). Excerpted by Bay Veterans of the Civil Rights Movement, http://www.crmvet.org.

21st century as not fully assuming adult responsibilities until their mid-thirties, it is sobering to remember that First Lady Jacqueline Kennedy was widowed by an assassin's bullet at 34 years old and that Reverend Dr. Martin Luther King, Jr. was 39 years old when he was assassinated.

At the international level, more than ten thousand unarmed Black school children from the township of Soweto, South Africa led a demonstration on June 17, 1976 to protest the imposition by the Bantu Education Department to use the Afrikaans language as the medium of instruction. Afrikaans was the language of white South Africans and was viewed as the language of the oppressor by Black South Africans. Two Black students were killed by police fire, Hastings Ndivou and Hector Pieterson. Sam Nzima's photo of a dying 13-year-old Hector landed on the front page of newspapers across the globe. Protests and boycotts continued across South Africa with Black and white students and adults expressing solidarity with the Soweto students.[4] The Soweto Student Uprisings are remembered as a turning point in the struggle to end the apartheid rule of South Africa.

The mainstream view of the 1968 SF State student strike is that it was part of the larger anti-war and student movements in the nation and around the world. While this is accurate, it is incomplete. For people of color, it hit close to home. It was personal and more appropriately viewed as part of the northern and western version of the Civil Rights Movement. As clearly articulated by SF State Emeritus professor Oba T'Shaka and others, the strike was part of the San Francisco Civil Rights Movement. Although American Indians, Latinos and Asian Americans predate Black people in the West and represent a smaller proportion of the population, Black people were the lead agents of change against the harsh treatment of people of color by white people. During World War II, the Black population had increased tenfold in San Francisco from 4,846 in 1940 to 43,502 by the 1950 Census and then to 74,833 in 1960.[5]

---

4 "Soweto Student Uprising," *South Africa: Overcoming Apartheid, Building Democracy*, http://overcomingapartheid.msu.edu/sidebar.php?id=65-258-3&page=1.

5 Jeffrey M. Burns, "Eugene Boyle, the Black Panther Party and the New Clerical Activism," *US Catholic Historian*, Vol 13. No. 3 (Summer 1995), 140, http://www.jstor.org/stable25254518.

"With the end of World War II, Blacks in San Francisco lost most of the jobs they held during the War. Shipyard jobs evaporated, and whites returning from the war replaced Blacks in many other jobs, leading to the Black unemployment rate rising to 30%. Once again Blacks were confined to nineteenth-century occupations as domestics, bootblacks, postal workers, longshoremen, and a few streetcar drivers. With the exception of ILWU (International Longshoremen and Warehousemen Union) jobs, union jobs were closed to Black people, leaving Black people and people of color invisible in the downtown economy. In the area of housing, as many as nine, ten, and fifteen people were crowded into a single room. The San Francisco Civil Rights Movement, which grew out of these dire economic conditions, was inspired by the Southern Civil Rights Movement, the Cuban Revolution, and the African Independence Movement. In 1960, Bob Slattery and Ella Hill Hutch formed the San Francisco branch of the Congress on Racial Equality (CORE). Ella Hill Hutch became the Mother of the San Francisco Civil Rights Movement and went on to become the first Black woman elected to the San Francisco Board of Supervisors."[6] Other people of color and white women also lost jobs to white men returning from the war. White women, by and large, were relegated to domestic work. The GI Bill favored education and housing in the suburbs and white husbands (then known as heads of household) who could support a housewife and family on one salary. This was not true of men of color in general with historic, chronic low-wage earnings and conditions that kept them stuck in the urban core or isolated in the rural fields.

SF State students were inspired by local Bay Area Black leaders, who focused on the larger community led by CORE. "In the 1960's under San Francisco CORE leadership, San Francisco CORE's central strength was that neither the white power structure, nor the Black elite had any control over the organization. CORE proved to be sell-out proof, and totally dedicated to the liberation of Black people and people of color. They were also smart: in the course of the San Francisco Civil Rights Movement they fought the economic power structure of San Francisco

---

6   Oba T'Shaka, "Africana Studies Department History: San Francisco State University," *The Journal of Pan African Studies*, vol. 5, no. 7 (October 2012), 15.

for jobs for Black and people of color because in their discussions with the Black grassroots, over and over again, Black folks said they needed jobs."[7] T'Oshaka went on to connect the experience of the San Francisco Civil Rights Movement as the learning ground for the 1964 Van Ness Auto Row demonstrations and the UC Berkeley Free Speech Movement. "The San Francisco Civil Rights Movement was the Mother Movement in the San Francisco Bay Area. Because many of the shock troops that took part in job demonstrations for over a year were University of California, Berkeley students, their radicalization inspired them to launch the Free Speech Movement. The San Francisco Civil Rights Movement gave birth to the Free Speech Movement. SFSU activists, who took part in the San Francisco Civil Rights Movement's Auto Row campaign, planned the San Francisco State Tutorial Program for Black youth in the Fillmore, in a jail cell, after they were arrested in the Auto Row sit-in. Lessons learned by these largely white students inspired them to form the Experimental College, where students were able to teach San Francisco State courses designed by students. The San Francisco Civil Rights Movement preceded the Black Panther Party, and provided inspiration to the Negro Student Association and the Black Student Union, which led to the San Francisco State Strike."[8] As founding TWLF and PACE leader and retired State Superior Court Judge Ron Quidachay noted, "The strike and the entire SFSU experience has been with me in all of that I have done. It has strengthened my understanding of commitment and compromise and the importance of community involvement and communication. I see the strike and the formation of ethnic studies and EOP as an important segment of the civil rights movement. They came about, as many rights and programs have, through the concerted endeavor and sacrifice of the concerned."[9]

---

7   Ibid., 15.
8   Ibid., 16.
9   "The People, the Soul of the Strike, A Work in Progress," https://ethnicstudies.sfsu.edu/sites/.../the%20people%2C%20the%20soul%20booklet.doc.

We Shall Overcome. We are Family.

Chapter 1 focused on the historical and cultural contexts of the young people who led the 1968 strike and developed the 1969 School of Ethnic Studies. These contexts placed the students in the right place at the right time, encouraging them to believe they would succeed. This is only part of the story. Success and achievement against the odds occurred in the face of adversity. Success and achievement occurred because students of color were taught by their communities that as non-white people, they had to be twice as good to get half as far as whites. They knew achievement was against the odds. At the same time, they were the lucky ones who knew that to whom much is given, much is expected. Review of mainstream media coverage during and after the strike reveals that it is rarely mentioned, and indeed often overlooked, that the initial TWLF students that went on strike entered SF State through regular admissions. We went to high schools like Galileo, Mission, Balboa, and Polytechnic, which were schools serving neighborhoods of lower-income whites and students of color, as well as academically-renowned public high schools such as Lowell and Washington, and private schools including St. Ignatius and Mercy. We could have chosen not to be involved with special admissions for students who were not as privileged. We could have been content to keep our campus and community lives separate. A campus life could be the road to a college degree and entry into middle class jobs and status, even a home in the suburbs. Nonetheless, a community life meant returning to younger brothers and sisters in inner city neighborhoods in need such as the Mission, Hunter's Point, the Bayview, Central City, the Fillmore and Chinatown.

My fellow strikers and I could make it. In fact, many did gain entry into the middle class and beyond. However, many also worried about the future of our little brothers and sisters. How long would the middle-class dream be available for children of color, especially those of working class backgrounds? They were not just our blood relatives. We knew and lived the reality shared by every child of color who had been taught by a dominant society to see himself or herself as less than equal; who were treated as subordinate, inferior, second class, marginal, invisible, except as deviants. One survival skill to counter such pervasive and demeaning daily experience was to cherish one another. Within the Black community, members addressed each other as brother and sister. In the pre-1965 Filipino American community, we were taught in the Ilocano tradition to say "Manong" and "Manang," meaning Older Brother and Older Sister. The Boys' Town motto, "He's not heavy, he's my brother," summarized the sibling bonds instilled by our parents and elders.

This came home to me in Fall 2007 when the leaders of the Filipino Cultural Association (FCA), a student organization of the University of Maryland, College Park approached me to help them establish a Filipino American Studies program. I had recently given a talk on campus about the establishment of not just Filipino American/Asian American Studies but also the College of Ethnic Studies at San Francisco State. President Jonathan Sterlin and vice president Ryan Herrera, both stellar seniors, already with job offers, documented for me how their younger siblings and cousins were falling through the cracks in Washington, DC, Baltimore, Baltimore County and Prince George's County. Despite the higher education and economic status of the DC area Filipino American community relative to the Bay Area, Jonathan and Ryan were concerned that, similar to the San Francisco Central City youth of 1968–1969, the DC-Baltimore area youth, in the beginning of the 21st century, were dropping out of high school and college, and headed to juvenile hall, prison or life on the streets. The FCA students were convinced that individually and organizationally, they had to show their younger siblings and cousins that positive alternatives existed, that college was accessible. These young people would find these alternatives by being knowledgeable about Filipino American history and meeting people of color who were role models and mentors. They did not leave my home until I agreed. Earlier in 1997, Asian American students led by Asian American Student Union president, Christina Lagdameo, had successfully fought for Asian Americans Studies. By spring, 2008, the first UMCP Filipino American courses were offered. In winter 2009, with adult community leaders, the Filipino Cultural Association student leaders were founding donors for the retired Army Major General Antonio M. Taguba Profiles in Courage and Leadership Scholarship.

Countering the dominant society's negative perspective on youth of color was the intellectual tradition and inner strength children of color honed in segregated schools and churches. In mainstream Protestant and Catholic houses of worship, youth of color were told that they were all God's children. They knew the Bible as oral and aural tradition and via Gospel or Gregorian choirs. Choir requires practice not just as an individual but as a team of different voices singing acapella or with musical instrumental accompaniment. The performance is for the congregation and the greater glory of God. In segregated schools, Black and other children of color learned the oratorical tradition, including the power of a good debate, which requires preparation, practice, research, the ability to anticipate your opponent's points, and calm delivery. Oratorical and musical performances were public performances with demonstrable results.

For white students, the call to serve beyond one's immediate family or community was poignantly made by a youthful President John F. Kennedy who challenged young Americans to ask what they could do for their country. Public service was defined as working in various communities, for example, by volunteering in other countries, such as in the Third World via the Peace Corps, where they provided technical assistance related to social and economic development. A domestic counterpart was VISTA, a national service program created to alleviate poverty in low-income neighborhoods, focusing on education and vocational training programs. After the president's 1963 assassination, his brother, Robert F. Kennedy, ran as a 1968 presidential candidate andexpanded the call to serve by reaching out to the coal mine workers in Appalachia and the farmworkers in the vineyards and fields of California. In the spirit of Reverend Martin Luther King Jr.'s call to respond not just to racism but also to poverty, as exemplified by the Poor People's March on Washington, Robert Kennedy urged American youth to address President Lyndon Johnson's War on Poverty.

In the Bay Area, young people of color understood that charity began at home. While mainstream media held negative portrayals of youth of color as deviants and criminals, the reality in communities of color in the late 1960s was that youth and young adults were serving their underserved communities as leaders and agents of change. In

Oakland, the Black Panther Party, under Huey Newton and Bobby Seale, became known not just as a political party but as a community center. In particular, community survival programs included the Panthers' Free Breakfast for Children, the Oakland Community School and other tutorial programs, free groceries, and free medical clinics. This perspective of thinking globally but acting locally across generations, especially in one's neighborhood, continues today. For example, a present counterpart of communities serving and protecting the vulnerable in their communities is the San Francisco-based violence prevention and youth development organization United Playaz in the South of Market (SoMa) neighborhood. Its founder, Rudy Corpuz, Jr., notes that United Playaz' motto is, "It Takes the Hood to Save the Hood." Stockton, CA Mayor Michael Tubbs, despite being born poor, Black, and male to a teenage mother and an incarcerated father, went on to great academic and career accomplishments with all sorts of opportunities. Instead of going out to the nation and world, he chose to go home to Stockton to work with his family, lifelong friends, and neighbors to address Stockton's problems, from racial disparities to economic resources.

The Importance of Community Colleges

In 2017, City College of San Francisco reverted back to being a public, accessible and tuition-free institution of higher education to persons living in San Francisco with established California residence, just as it was in 1968–69. The importance of community colleges, especially for people of color and the working class, must be acknowledged. Community colleges are public and inclusive, drawing most of their students from immediate residents and obtaining funding from local resources. Historically it has been an affordable path for many residents to upward mobility, through transfer to four-year colleges and universities. Furthermore, community colleges with long-term relationships to business communities provides skilled labor for local and other industries, thus ensuring a competent, stable workforce, good paying jobs, and a middle class. In the 1960s, they were also called junior colleges (two years with Associate Degrees and the ability to transfer to state college and universities for Bachelor and other degrees). For a good portion of SF State students, especially people of color, many had transferred from City College of San Francisco and other junior colleges.

Community college students were active in supporting the strike at San Francisco State and the demand for a College of Third World Studies. In particular, Black students at Laney Junior College and Merritt Community College (initially Oakland City College), of the Peralta Community College District, had already led the way with Black Studies curriculum at their institutions in the mid-1960s. Merritt College was the meeting place for Black Panther Party leaders. Furthermore, BSU leaders from a number of San Francisco Bay Area colleges, including San Francisco State College and City College of San Francisco, held open forums in off campus communities, with an emphasis upon reaching Black high school students. One such forum, sponsored by the organization Plan of Action for Challenging Times (PACT), was held at Polytechnic High School in San Francisco. At this forum, a number of BSU presidents, including Benny Stewart of SF State and Larry Pinkney of CCSF, explained the necessity for the struggles at both colleges, the need for a "revolutionary black philosophy," and the role of Black high school students could play in the movement.[10]

According to Pinkney, "Of the hundreds of Black college students at CCSF, many, including Anna Barry, Derrick Hill, Jerry L. King III, and myself were organizing on campus, in our determination to press the CCSF administration to 1) establish an accredited Afro American Studies Department, 2) hire Black instructors and administrators, and 3) to create a Black history section in the college library."[11] The CCSF BSU worked with La Raza Unida, Chinese Voice Party, SDS and Samoan allies on and off campus for a CCSF student strike to show solidarity with the SF State strike. In the late 1960s, CCSF also supported tutoring programs with its students assisting San Francisco elementary students in low-income neighborhoods. Students and tutor coordinators worked

10   "Fiery Black Meeting at Poly High," *San Francisco Chronicle*, December 20, 1968, http://www.blackactivistwg.org/blog/fiery-black-meeting-at-poly-high.
11   Larry Pinkney, "The San Francisco State Strike: Students at City College of San Francisco, the Impact of the Black Panther Party," http://www.itsabouttimebpp.com/Student_Support/The_San_Francisco_State_Strike.html.

with the Black Panthers at Sacred Heart Church and the Brown Berets in the Mission Coalition. As the Haight Ashbury tutor coordinator, fellow students and I worked with multiethnic and multiracial students and their families.

The Student Strikers and Activists

The following examples are illustrative, not exhaustive, of the young people of the United States who stood up with courage and determination at a pivotal time in the nation's history.

After the massive arrests of January, 1969, this observation was offered by the Research Organizing Committee:

> "We all owe a tremendous debt to the strike at SF State. First of all, the resolution of its demands should benefit all Third World and white origin people, by opening the college to the people who most need it and the courses they need. Second, the strike has been a model for similar movements all over the country. And third, the strike has exposed the true nature of the State and the law. If we learn what the strike has brought into the open, and identify our common enemies, we will be able to fight for the rest of what we need. Change will not be effortless, but nothing worth fighting for is easy.

> "As we learn these lessons, we cannot forget the people who have done the fighting for us. The arrested strikers were not fighting for their own advantage. They were already in college. They could have "made it," just by keeping their mouths shut, but they stuck their necks out for the common good. Now they need lawyers. They need your support. And they need your money. Support the arrested strikers, and you support yourself."[12]

Connell Joe Persico was one of the early student leaders well versed in organizing work, having participated in the 1961 anti-House Un-

---

12   Research Organizing Cooperative of San Francisco, *Strike at Frisco State! The story behind it* (San Francisco: Research Organizing Cooperative of San Francisco, 1969).

American Activities Committee (HUAC) demonstrations, the Southern Freedom Rides in the 1960s, and the 1964 UC Berkeley Free Speech Movement. He served as SF State student body president during 1964–65 and was involved in various SF State academic innovations, including in 1965, the Community Involvement Program (CIP) and Experimental College, in 1966, Black Studies courses and the Work Study Program, in 1967 the Media Innovations Institute and the Center for Educational Innovation, and in 1968, the Special Admissions Program/Educational Opportunity Program and Division of Area Ethnic Studies. He succinctly summarized the 1968–69 strike, "is the result of 5 years of failure to resolve who should govern campus and to whom should governors be responsible."[13]

On November 18, 1968, the California State Board of Trustees held an emergency meeting in Los Angeles on the SF State strike. Various students addressed the trustees. "Russell Bass, SF State student body president, told them that there had been no 'program of education' taking place at San Francisco State College since the strike began, and that it would be impossible for students to return to class, 'as long as the problems which created the tensions are present.' Rather than worrying so much about reopening the college, Bass suggested that it might be better if they attempted to 'supply the necessary resources and funds that San Francisco State must have if we are to provide equal and relevant education for third world students.'"[14]

Victor Lee was another student who spoke at the trustees meeting: "The last student allowed to speak was Victor Lee, the student body president at San Jose State College who was also president of the California State College Student Presidents Association (CCSPA), an organization which officially represented all for the students in the state college system at the Trustees' meetings. Lee outlined what he perceived to be the 'sickness' of the state college system, specifically citing its callousness toward minority groups, its 'toleration of outside

---

13 Connell Persico, "A Crisis in Governance: A Case Study of San Francisco State College: 1962 – 1966" in San Francisco State University Strike Collection, Sharon Martinas Collection, box 19, folder 158, item 2.
14 Barlow and Shapiro, 234-5.

political intervention' in its affairs, and its perpetuation of 'a superfluous outmoded concept of curriculum' . . . 'If you open the campus by any means necessary,' he said, referring to one of Governor Reagan's public statements, 'you will simply be no more right than those who say they will close that campus by any means necessary.'"[15]

Lee was born in Shanghai, China and raised in Tokyo, Japan. In his own words: "My dad was a well-known foreign correspondent, author and TV commentator who was assigned to Japan during the occupation after World War II. My mom was a Chinese opera actor. So, I guess television and journalism is in my DNA. I came to the states for college as a foreign student after graduating from the American school in Japan. I attended San Jose State during the turbulent 60's. In 1964, during the height of the Vietnam War and civil rights protests, I was elected student body president. I learned a lot about politics and activism through that experience. I started my career in journalism with an internship at the *New York Times*, and then joined United Press International (UPI) in 1969, where I served in Portland, Tokyo and Los Angeles."[16]

George Woo, who initially worked with Chinatown youth, including the Wah Ching, came on campus as a concerned community member during the strike. Graduating from Galileo High School in 1956, he joined the Navy between the Korean War and Vietnam War and trained in aviation and electronics. Over the years, he became known for 1) the Asian American Studies consensus model (not majority rule) established in the Asian American Studies Planning Committee, 2) facilitating Asian American/Ethnic Studies courses to fulfill general education graduation requirements, hence institutionalizing the studies within academia and advocating for the university to send students back to serve their communities, and 3) viewing Ethnic Studies as interdisciplinary.[17]

In her own words, Donna Amador noted, "It was the fall of 1968 and I had just returned from the Poor People's Campaign, a trek to Washington, D.C. I brought back home many ideas for making changes in my world.

---

15   Barlow and Shapiro, 235.
16   Vic Lee, "Vic Lee," *ABC 7 News*, http://abc7news.com/about/newsteam/vic-lee.
17   George Woo, interview with author, June 7, 2017.

I was in my last year at San Francisco State University (SFSU). For the first time, I was employed at the university instead of going to school in the morning and working in an office in the afternoon. To be involved full time in school and political activities was an incredible opportunity for me. I was serving as secretary for the Third World Liberation Front (TWLF), a mix of Chicano, Latino, Asian, American Indian and African-American campus organizations. Within the TWLF, we had a chance to know each other and collaborate on some projects, but it was the fight of ethnic studies and an enrollment polity that would allow admission of more ethnic minorities that united us all in the fall of 1968. Our demands were not outrageous; admission of more minorities to SFSU, creation of an actual ethnic studies department, and some respect for the rights of minorities on campus. Several departments were trying to present classes that included our history, art, and other contributions, but institutionally we didn't exist. We were at a strictly "Western Civilization" and "Important White Male Authors/Philosophers/Artists" University, regardless of how much we lobbied and protested."[18]

Anita Sanchez was a 19 year-old sophomore and graduate of Balboa High School when she came up to me in the hallway of the HSS building asking about PACE and how she could join the strike line. Ten years earlier, her US Navy veteran dad had brought his family to the US from the Philippines. Multilingual in various Philippine dialects and English, Anita was concerned that young people of color, particularly new immigrants in the Balboa School District, Potrero Hill, the Mission and Central City were dropping out of high school, many headed for the Youth Guidance Center (known as Juvie) or being drafted for the Vietnam War. With community activists and ethnic studies supporters Jimmy Queen and Tom Kim, she worked with hundreds of youth in RAP, the Real Alternative Program.[19] After earning a social worker degree and years of volunteer work, Anita held critical positions in the

---

18   Donna Amador, "Third World Liberation and the Rise of Latino Power," in *The Whole World's Watching: Peace and Social Justice Movements of the 1960s & 1970s* (Berkeley: Berkeley Center Association, 2001), 83.

19   "Assignment Four: We'll Do it Ourselves," *Bay Area Television Archive*, https://diva.sfsu.edu/collections/sfbatv/ bundles/210743.

San Francisco city government from Mayor Dianne Feinstein to Mayor Edwin Lee, initiating many social service programs and institutions in the South of Market area, including a building to Ed de la Cruz, fellow striker and social worker.

Strikers Interviewed during 40th Anniversary Commemoration
On October 29 - November 1, 2008, San Francisco State University commemorated the 40th anniversary of the 1968 SF State Black Student Union/Third World Liberation Front student-led Strike. This was a few days before the historic election of the first Black president of the United States, Barack H. Obama. SF State noted the occasion with an article, stating:

> "Many SF State strike alumni rose to prominence in the fields of social justice, law, public health, education and public service. They include actor and activist Danny Glover, who was a member of the Black Student Union, and California Superior Court Judge Ronald Quidachay, who worked on the strike as a member of the Philippine American College Endeavor (PACE) and was a TWLF spokesperson. Alumnus and statesman Willie Brown, then a young lawyer and legislator, worked to free striking students who were jailed, as did, former Congressman, Oakland Mayor and alumnus Ron Dellums."

Of the strikers who chose public education as a career, several returned to SF State as faculty including Associate Dean of the College of Ethnic Studies and the Graduate School of Education Laureen Chew, Professor of Asian American Studies Dan Gonzales, and Professor of Raza Studies Roberto Rivera.[20] In his welcoming letter in the conference program, then university president Robert Corrigan noted:

> "Throughout the course of this conference, you will hear testimony about how the student-led strike of 1968 at San Francisco State changed this campus and opened doors to not only students and faculty of color, but to a broad range of men

---

20 "Campus commemorates 1968 student-led strike," *SFSU*, http://www.sfsu.edu/news/2008/fall/8.html.

and women who had been excluded or overlooked in higher education. Forty years later, we look back on a time of strife and sacrifice to say unequivocally that fundamental changes to higher education have resulted, opening the doors to perspectives, peoples and approaches that had been excluded.

"I was not here at the time of the strike, but I can say first-hand that it had a national impact. At the time, I was on the American Studies faculty at the University of Iowa and we saw this extraordinary movement spreading from SF State across America: the notion that we needed to open up universities, expand the curriculum, and study the contributions of ethnic and national minority groups to our nation's history and society. That is when the president of the University of Iowa program decided that we should establish a black studies department, and asked me to start the program. SF State paved the way. Within a decade of that historic strike, the Iowa program would be just one of more than 8,000 offerings in ethnic studies offered by more than 430 colleges and universities."[21]

Throughout 3 days of formal ceremonies, organized panels, and spontaneous reunions, the 1968 student and faculty strikers were interviewed by current 2008 students, including undergraduate and graduate students, as well as native San Franciscans and brand new immigrants. These interviews are part of the San Francisco State Archives.[22]

It is interesting to note that even after forty years, the interviewees did not articulate going to college for self-actualization and careers as much as an educational tool to improve the human condition. They still spoke of relevant education to meet the needs of working class communities. In keeping with the low, almost humble demeanor of any

---

21 Robert A. Corrigan, "Office of the President," *SFSU*, http://
ethnicstudies.sfsu.edu/sites/default/files/assets/downloads/40th%20
StrikeConf%20Final%20Program2.pdf
22 "Roger Alvarado Interview," *SFSU*, https://diva.sfsu.edu/collections/
coes/bundles/218230.

permanent memorial to this period, there is a huge rock that says, "1968 . . . 2008 / Connect the dots."

In addition to the interviews, the commemoration organizers and Archive Committee of the 40th Commemoration released a booklet, *The People, the Soul of the Strike, A Work in Progress*, which asked strike veterans to speak on their role in the strike, their personal sacrifices, and what resonates most today. John Levin, then a member of the Progressive Labor Party and SDS, noted that "SDS's role in the strike was to organize the white students in solidarity with the BSU/TWLF demands—in much the same way unions strike in solidarity with other unions. Our strategy was to build a broad united front in which all who supported the strike could participate at whatever level their 'comfort zone' allowed."[23]

Mason Wong, who was president of the Intercollegiate Chinese Student Association (ICSA), noted that the college's pre-strike special admissions program was for athletes and legacy candidates, benefitting students whose families were already in the system. "We wanted, instead, to get more people into the system whose families were not already in the system. My experiences at SF State helped me become much more aware of problems all over the world. And even now, when I see strikers holding picket signs, I always honk!"[24]

Roger Alvarado, who is perhaps the most visible spokesperson for the TWLF strike, noted that he hadn't been back on campus in over forty years. After the strike settlement, like other arrested strikers, he had to address his charges and move on with life off campus. He returned to community work on a range of issues, including the publicized Los Siete de La Raza Defense Committee. Despite the greater representation of people of color at SF State since 1969, young people, especially young men, continued to be in contentious conditions of survival in low income and people of color communities. Los Siete were seven young Latinos from the Mission—Salvadoran, Nicaraguan, and Honduran—who were arrested and tried for the murder of San Francisco Police officer Joe Brodnik and the attempted murder of his fellow plainclothesman officer Paul McGoran. Defended by civil rights attorney Charles Garry

23 *The People, the Soul of the Strike, A Work in Progress*, 12.
24 *The People, the Soul of the Strike, A Work in Progress*, 25.

84

and drawing from the support of student and community activists, the young men were acquitted. Roger noted that many people stepped up to the plate at SF State. It was a rare, defining moment for people to come together.[25] Roger was one of the first 1968–69 TWLF strikers to come on campus and show solidarity with the 2016 TWLF strikers.

Roberto Vargas was born in Nicaragua in 1941 under the Somoza dictatorship. His family immigrated to San Francisco first to the Bayview District in project housing then moved to the Fillmore and Mission. Not knowing English, he looked forward to Latino films that were screened in the Fillmore. Like many upwardly mobile lower income and people of color, Roberto attended City College of San Francisco and served in the United States Marine Corps. An active organizer in the arts and poetry community, he came on campus during the strike to add his support and networks.[26] He went on to be a creative writing lecturer in La Raza Studies and a writer for *El Tecolote*, the bilingual Latino community newspaper that began as a project in La Raza Studies at SF State in August, 1970 under founder and first editor Juan Gonzales. The paper continues to thrive with a largely volunteer staff, including college students and young journalists.

Jacob Perea was on his way from Half Moon Bay to SF State to interview for a master's program when police surrounded Junipero Serra Boulevard. He had just returned from serving in the Peace Corps in Africa. Undaunted, Jacob continued with his graduate degrees and commitment to social justice through education.[27] He became active in education community service, including recruiting young people from racial/ethnic neighborhoods. He was acting chair for American Indian Studies and La Raza Studies. He developed the SF State Bilingual Teacher Training Program and Step to College Program, a collaborative project with SFUSD to provide access for under-represented groups in higher education. Jacob retired as the first American Indian (Mescalero Apache)

---

25 "Roger Alvardo Interview," *SFSU COES* video, 12:05, https://diva.sfsu. edu/collections/coes/bundles/218230.
26 "Roberto Vargas Interview," *SFSU COES* video, 1:23:51, https://diva. sfsu.edu/collections/coes/bundles/218229.
27 "Jacob Perea Interview," *SFSU COES* video, 9:05, https://diva.sfsu.edu/ collections/coes/bundles/218216.

Dean of the Graduate College of Education.

Sharon Gold Martinas entered campus in fall 1964. She was a graduate student from an upper middle class white background. Before the BSU and TWLF were formed, she worked with Roger Alvarado and Joe Persico, the 1964 -65 student body president and co-founder of the Experimental College, to set up tutorial and work study programs in San Francisco communities of color. She worked with faculty to provide academic credit for community work by students. In 1965, Roger Alvarado had written a proposal calling for low-income high school students (disproportionately of color) to be admitted to SF State. This became the basis of the Educational Opportunity Program (EOP), which was part of the strike demands. As the strike progressed, Sharon Gold Martinas assumed leadership in the Legal Defense Committee to ensure that attention was focused on arrested students, faculty and community and to raise bail bonds. Much of her personal collection for this period was donated to the San Francisco State Strike Archives Collection.

Dharmeera Ahmad, aka Carlotta Simon, was fresh out of high school and one of the first EOP students at SF State in 1968. She was an active member of the BSU and Black Panther Party. She was instrumental in implementing the common goal of the SF State strikers and the Black Panthers to serve the needs of their local communities, especially the youth, by participating in BSU meetings with Black communities in San Francisco and the Bay Area.[28] She went on to teach in the Oakland Unified School District, retiring as a principal.

Another inspiring teenager during the strike was Penny Nakatsu, who graduated a year after me from Morning Star School. She was one of the very few women on the TWLF Central Committee. Via the Asian American Political Alliance, first at UC Berkeley and then at SF State, Penny, along with Paul Yamazaki, eloquently articulated the importance of Asian Americans taking a stand beyond our Asian ethnic groups— Chinese, Filipino, Japanese, Korean—in solidarity with other people of color in the city and around the world. At that point, the Japanese American community was beginning to flex its power. With courageous

---

28 "Dhameera Ahmad Interview," *SFSU COES* video, 20:12, https://diva.
sfsu.edu/collections/coes/bundles/218203.

leaders like Edison Uno, who was one of the pioneer SF State Ethnic Studies faculty, the community began breaking the silence of the Japanese American internment during World War II. Along with Edison Uno, Yori Wada, and others, Penny was instrumental in organizing the Asian American, especially Japanese American, communities to protest the appointment, policies, and practices of SF State interim president S.I. Hayakawa.

TWLF 2016 Strike

In 2016, the College of Ethnic Studies at SF State was in jeopardy and was struggling to accomplish its mission due to impending major budget cuts. On March 8, the San Francisco State University chapter of the California Faculty Association adopted a resolution that, "fully supports the rights of students to obtain a quality affordable public education; demand complete transparency of the allocation of funding on the state, CSU, university and college level; and demand full funding for the College of Ethnic Studies and all other colleges on campus." This resolution occurred with no immediate follow up. Not surprisingly, SF State students took the lead and again went on strike. As in 1968–1969, there were similar protests at other campuses in California and across the nation to defend and advance the interests of students of color in 2016, especially the ability to obtain and afford a public state college education.

In addition to San Francisco State, the UC and California State University systems were still reeling from budget cuts since the Great Recession of 2008–2009 and the increasing enrollment of California youth in higher education, especially children of color. When *Agents of Change* premiered on May 15, 2016 at the Castro Theater, the 1968 and 1969 strikers, activists, and their supporters had a poignant reunion with the younger generations. Equally important, younger activists were heartened, especially those who had taken ethnic studies and/or been recipients and beneficiaries of the various types of programs created by or coming about as a consequence of the SF State strike and the College of Ethnic Studies.

Earlier that month, on May 4, 2016, with then COES Dean Ken Monteiro, co-producers and directors Abby Ginzberg and Frank

Dawson arranged an on-campus screening of *Agents of Change* for SF State students, faculty, and staff. It was followed by a panel discussion with Ginzberg, Dawson and TWLF 1968-69 strikers in the film—Benny Stewart, Jimmy Garrett, Ramona Tascoe, and me—with four current undergraduate COES students known as the TWLF 2016 strikers. They were Hassani Bell, Ahkeel Mestayer, Julia Retzlaff, and Sachiel Rosen. The 1968–69 students were humbled by the 2016 student leaders, who went beyond past tactics and initiated a hunger strike to protest the cuts. Mestayer, a junior, who came up with the idea to have the hunger strike, was quoted as saying, "These programs changed my life. They benefitted me: made me a better person. I felt that this was something I was willing to put my body on the line for."[29] These young people again saw the importance of the campus to be relevant not just to their academic needs but to the communities from which they came and would go back to serve. The 2016 students were supported by 1968–69 student leaders including Danny Glover and Roger Alvarado, now fathers and grandfathers, who came on campus to stand with the students. The 2016 TWLF strikers made the connection of legacy across generations. They ended their 10-day hunger strike with a significant win and lesson. Right before the May 15 premiere of *Agents of Change* at the Castro Theater, the four students met with SFSU President Leslie Wong who signed an agreement on May 11, committing almost half-a-million dollars over-and-beyond an immediate shortfall needed to help fund SFSU's chronically underfunded College of Ethnic Studies. Like the demands of the 1968–69 strikers, the demands of the 2016 TWLF strikers were not all met. Nonetheless, restored funds were crucial to ensure the continuation of the College of Ethnic Studies. While many other universities host ethnic studies departments and programs following SFSU's led, SF State remains the only school in the nation to have a college dedicated to the cultures and histories of people of color and to stress that the university serve communities. Just as almost 50 years earlier when support for the 1968–69 strike came from across the US and other nations, the 2016

---

29 Jack Herrera, "10-Day Hunger Strike = Victory for SFSU Students," *USA Today College*, May 22, 2016, http://college.usatoday.com/2016/05/22/10-day-hunger-strike-victory-for-sfsu-students.

TWLF strike was equally acknowledged. "Our support was international in scope," noted Andrew Jolivette, then chair of the American Indian Studies Department. Jolivette, along with various other faculty members in the College of Ethnic Studies, supported the strikers and worked with the group on strategy.[30]

In my view, the success of the 2016 TWLF Strike reaffirmed at least two bonds. One was that the adults and communities off campus promptly and visibly supported their children, just as during the 1968–69 strike. Intergenerational bonds were renewed and signified that advocating for education for all our children endured across communities and is not limited to time and place. Parents and grandparents expect the best for their children and grandchildren and will sacrifice along with them. Second is that the 2016 strike re-energized young people, especially of color and in immigrant communities, demonstrating that children and youth can lead and win. *As Agents of Change* shows, the backlash against ethnic studies at all levels of education in the last decades has been chilling. The resentment and resistance against youth-led movements like Black Lives Matter and youth-specific initiatives such as the Deferred Action for Childhood Arrivals (DACA) executive order continue.

Nonetheless, young people and their supporters stay the course. For example, that summer on July 14, I was at the California State Board of Education in Sacramento with fellow SF State PACE and strike alumni and military veterans, Roderick de la Conception and Ray Cordova, to testify as members of the Bataan Legacy Historical Society for the inclusion of the Bataan Death March and World War II in the Pacific for the 11th grade history and social science curriculum framework in

---

30 "2016 Student Demonstrations and Hunger Strike," http://ethnicstudies. sfsu.edu/content/2016-student-demonstrations-and-hunger-strike; Labor Video Project, *SFSU TWLF 2016 Hunger Striker's Demands At May 9, 2016 Rally*, 2016 YouTube Video, 7:54, posted by "laborvideo," May 10, 2016, https://www.youtube.com/watch?v=umgRO_Hwqgg; Labor Video Project, *Danny Glover Speaks Out In Support Of SF State Ethnic Studies Hunger Strikers*, 2016 YouTube Video, 7:25, posted by "laborvideo," May 9, 2016, https:// www.youtube.com/watch?v=G965nQn_g1E; *Hunger strike demands attention from President Wong*, 2016 YouTube Video, 2:12, posted by "Xpress News," May 12, 2016, https://www.youtube.com/watch?v=S_aDhbzUh9c.

California public schools. We arrived very early, around 7:30 a.m., hoping to beat the crowd. To our surprise, we found the lobby and first floor of the education building overflowing with elementary, middle, and high school students from Stockton and parts of central California. By buses and cars, they had come with teachers, staff and parents to present their two-minutes each of testimony on the importance of ethnic studies in their curriculum and classrooms and for their existence and life chances.

The life chances for American children continue to be problematic; inadequate resources for ethnic studies in 2016 is just the beginning. There is no end in sight to the shooting and killing of our children in the 21st century. From shootings in elementary schools, including Sandy Hook Elementary in Newtown CT on December 14, 2012 to high schools, including Marjory Stoneman Douglas High School in Parkland, FL on February 18, 2018, the expectation that our youth will go to college is not to be taken for granted. Their ability to grow up to be adults cannot be taken for granted. On March 24, 2018, middle schoolers and highs schoolers led rallies and marches in hundreds of cities in the US and abroad that were attended by hundreds of thousands of people. They asked: can they expect to even reach voting age if they cannot depend on adults to ensure that they can live? Given this state of affairs, young people are not only becoming more vocal and active in asking why adults are not caring for the children—they are running for office and winning.

As highlighted in a 2017 article, there were several millennial generation politicians that year, including 27-year-old Michael Tubbs, mayor of Stockton, CA, who noted that, "Government is not designed to move fast. . . . If you prototype something and it fails, it's just an internal conversation in your office. If I prototype water delivery or trash, it touches everyone, especially the most vulnerable." Pete Buttigieg was 35 years old in 2017 and was elected mayor of South Bend, Indiana at 29 years old. He observed, "Ours might be the first generation of mayors who don't necessarily consider state and federal government a step up. A generation ago, folks like us wouldn't run for local office in the first place—we would go to law school, try to work for a Congressman and then try to be a Congressman."[31] In early 2018, the Washington Post

---

31   Charlotte Alter, "When Millennials Rule," *Time*, October 23, 2017.

reported that several teenagers in Kansas were running for governor and that such an idea did not seem so preposterous.[32] It may be another historical instance when the children lead because the adults do not.

The Legacy of Alcatraz

Perhaps the most publicized connection of youth activism on campus and in the broader community emanating from the 1968–69 strike and fight for ethnic studies was the occupation of Alcatraz. In the summer of 1969, planning of the various ethnic studies courses and departments was underway not just at SF State, but several Bay Area and southern California campuses. Native American students, while smaller in number than other students of color, were a powerful presence and inspiration. At SF State, Richard Oakes was the most prominent.[33]

At UC Berkeley, La Nada Means (LaNada War Jack) served a similar role. In the prior decade, the federal Indian Relocation Act of 1956 encouraged American Indians to move from tribal lands into urban areas for resettlement and assimilation. This was in keeping with the US policy of Indian termination. Native peoples protested and the historical occupation of Alcatraz was the most visible act of resistance. In 1963, Alcatraz was closed as a federal penitentiary and became surplus federal property. The first attempted occupation of Alcatraz as Indian Land followed shortly after the closure. On March 8, 1964, the attempted occupation was led by several Sioux Indians with a few supporters and media. They claimed the island based on the right to seize surplus federal land. They called for the building of an Indian university and cultural center. However, the Sioux did not have ancestral claim in San Francisco and were removed by federal authorities after several hours. The second occupation, led by Indian college students from SF State and other colleges and the Indians of All Tribes groups was longer, lasting over 18 months from November 20, 1969 to June 11, 1971. This occupation was poignant not only because of the student demands for

---

32   Monica Hesse, "Six teenagers are running for governor in Kansas, and suddenly this doesn't seem so preposterous," *Washington Post*, March 2, 2018.
33   "Voices of Promise and Protest Exploring the Activism of Native Peoples during the 1968 SF State Strike," *SFSU COES*, 1:28:38, https://diva.sfsu.edu/collections/coes/bundles/218250.

self-determination and relevant education but because on October 28, 1969, a fire had destroyed the San Francisco Indian Center. American Indian Studies Professor Troy Johnson of California State University, Long Beach, observed, "The success or failure of the occupation should not be judged by whether the demand for title to the island was realized. The underlying goal of the Indians on Alcatraz Island was to awaken the American public to the plight of the first Americans, to the suffering caused by the federal government's broken treaties and broken promises, and to the need for Indian self-determination. In this the occupiers were indeed successful. As a result of the Alcatraz occupation, either directly or indirectly, the official US government policy of termination of Indian tribes was ended, replaced by a policy of Indian self-determination."[34] The Red Power Movement manifested in the occupation of Alcatraz from 1969–71 and deeply informed SF State's Native American Studies program (later American Indian Studies), just as the Black Power Movement shaped the early years of Black Studies (later Africana Studies). The home page for SF State's American Indian Studies Department notes, "Their vision was based on a commitment to community participation and service —from the community to campus and from the campus to the community —towards the goal of facilitating American Indian self-determination through education."[35]

In 2018, Alcatraz is part of the National Park Service. The connection of Alcatraz to American Indians is now a daily visible educational experience in part due to the young activists at SF State and other campuses fifty years ago. Various tribes throughout the Americas—North, Central and South—gather annually to hold ceremonies on Indigenous People's Day and Thanksgiving Day with sunrise gatherings attended by thousands of people. The starlit night makes way to the soft pinks and yellows of sunrise, accompanied by birds overhead, drumming, chanting, and the passing of sage peace pipes. Visitors can see the huge water tower with signs painted in red including: "Peace and Freedom," "Welcome to Indian Land," and "Home of the Free Indian."

While I was on a tour of Alcatraz Gardens in summer 2017, I met

---

34 Troy Johnson, "The Occupation of Alcatraz," *IPOAA Magazine*, n.d.
35 "American Indian Studies (AIS)," *SFSU*, https://sfsuais.sfsu.edu.

one of the park volunteers, a former SF State alumnus, Gerry Wright, who told me that the water tower is re-painted regularly by American Indians.[36] He suggested I confirm this with another volunteer, Dick Miner. I assumed the original painting was done by the young activists of 1969–1971. I asked Dick if they were part of the post 1971 painters, along with grandchildren. He wrote, "Yes. The political statement, repainters of the water tower, were composed of the original painters . . . just 45 years older. There was one grandson whose name is Isaiah that was part of the paint restoration crew. He now (sic) a regular and was just out with Eloi Martinez and the others to do some work up by the cell house. He is probably in his twenties and has been very involved in much of their recent civil rights activity. He often speaks at the Thanksgiving sunrise activities."[37] This intergenerational ritual is life-affirming, a physical passing of history from one generation to its children and grandchildren.

Another form of passing down and sharing legacy occurred on February 11, 2018 at the reception honoring Professor Kenneth Monteiro for his twelve years as Dean of the College of Ethnic Studies. These were two affirmations of *e pluribus unum*. One was the vibrant and united presence of the 1968 strikers, the Golden Children—both white and people of color—reaffirming the importance of the successful fight for and endurance of ethnic studies across generations and community. Secondly, as a multigenerational event, it was the affirmation of the power of children and youth to be leaders whether it be in 1968 or 2018 or beyond.

Before the end of the 20th century, US Census Bureau demographers projected that people of color were increasing numerically and proportionally. In the 21st century, the demography of SF State, California and the US depict a growing population of students in higher education, many who are people of color and/or immigrants. The younger Millennial Cohort of the 2016 TWLF strikers is larger than the 1968 Baby Boomer Cohort. As recorded in the decennial censuses since the 1980 Census, the US is increasingly becoming not just a greater mixed-race population but also more mobile, more migrant, and more urbanized.

---

36   Gerry Wright, personal communication with author, July 21, 2017.
37   Dick Miner, personal communication with author, July 21, 2017.

IN MEMORIAM
From 40th anniversary—the people, the soul booklet: [38]

Dharmeera Ahmad (Carlotta Simon)
John Alcorn
Ron Bentley
Joe Bill
Rich Bliss
Liz Dewitt Belcher
Carolina Borromeo
Kaye Boyle
Franklin Brann
Art Carraway
Aug Malonga Casquelord
Chinosole "Pat Thorton"
Phillip P. Choy
Woesha Cloud North
Flournoy Coles
Nia Carol Cornwell
Jesus Contreras
Elmer Cooper
Ed De La Cruz
Gordon De Marco
William Dickey
Jeff Freed
Tom Gable
Isidro Gali
Velia Garcia Hancock
John 'Tito' Gerassi
Brenda Goodman
Paula Gunn Allen
Laura Head
James Hirabayashi

---

38 https://ethnicstudies.sfsu.edu/content/memorium and author.

Bernard Hoehner 'Peji'
Mary Rhodes Hoover
John Ihle
Khosoro Kalantari
Louie Kemnitzer
Vernon Ketcheshawno
Syed Khatib
Tom Kim
Mickey Kimmel
Mark Him Lai
Mary Lewis
Reginald Lockett
Reginald Majors "Reggie"
Enola Maxwell
D. Phillip Mcgee
Bevelyn Ann Moss
Ted Murguia
Sachiko Nakamura
Donna Nomura
Richard Oakes
Frances Oka
Juan Pifare
George Price
Robert Prudhomme
Julian Richardson
Rebecca Rubi
Claire Sallop
Tim Sampson
Anita Sanchez
Carl Lee Sanchez
Kurt Schneider
Tomatra Scott
Randy Senzaki
Pat Sumi
Fred Thalheimer

Philip Tingley
James Todd
Helen Toribio
Edison Uno
Ahlerman Vann Lewis
Felicissimo 'Moy' Velasquez
Sid Welch
Herbert Williams
Herbert Wilner
James Dudley Yasuda[39]

---

39 This is unlikely to be a comprehensive list. Names submitted include those from for the College of Ethnic Studies, San Francisco State University 46th Anniversary Celebration, November 8, 2015.

CHAPTER 4

Demography Is Destiny But Geography Shapes Outlook

In 1968, the SF State strike made visible to the world the possibilities of a multiracial, multiethnic, multilingual and more globally aware community. It may be a microcosm of how things can turn out. It is an example of the American motto, *E pluribus unum*. Yale scholar Amy Chua and other researchers note there have been other, not necessarily many, examples in American history of "From many, one." The integration of the US military is cited as a very successful model. On the eve of the United States' entry into World War II, President Franklin Roosevelt signed Executive Order 8802 prohibiting racial discrimination in employment in the national defense industry. This order was followed by Executive Order 9981 issued by President Harry Truman on July 26, 1948, which abolished racial discrimination in the US Armed Forces. It established a policy of "equality of treatment and opportunity for all persons in the armed services without regard to race, color, religion or national origin." The integration of major league baseball is another example of inclusion of minority groups in order to have a more representative nation. This integration was quickly followed by the expansion of baseball teams west of the Mississippi. Major league baseball became more successful and popular, not only drawing a wider audience, but also inspiring youngsters of every color to be in sports. Yet a third example is a 21st century one. Since 2001, DiversityInc has issued a list of the top 50 companies for diversity. CNBC reporter, Betha Cooms noted, "The companies that compete to earn a spot on the DiversityInc Top 50—and the specialty lists—understand the importance of diverse workforces and management teams. Research shows that the most diverse companies tend to actually perform better financially than the overall market."[1]

---

1 Ellen McGirt, "For These 50 companies, Diversity means Success," *Fortune*, May 4, 2017, http://fortune.com/2017/05/04/for-these-50-companies-diversity-means-success/.

Yet, in 2018 there is very visible backlash, not only against racial and ethnic minorities, but any group in a subordinate status, including women, disabled folks, the LGBT community, poor people and American youth and children. An anti-immigration climate endures despite the fact that the existence and economic power of Silicon Valley is in large part due to a workforce of immigrants and their children. The labor force needs of the US for low- and high-skilled foreigners, along with the various wars since World War II that contributed to war-related kin and refugees immigrating to the US, are primary factors in the changing face of the United States from white to golden.

As it turns 50 years old, the challenge and opportunity for the College of Ethnic Studies at SF State is not to just remain relevant but to continue leading the way to ensure access to higher education, to nurture a competitive labor force, to graduate responsible citizens, and to serve the public good. How does it provide value amidst changes in the role, expectations and return on investment to higher education? To be blunt, how does the college present a win-win situation in a campus, state, and nation that is more and more demographically golden in the face of a threatened White minority? One way to address these questions is to examine the interplay of demography and geography. The BSU/TWLF-led strikers and supporters of the College of Ethnic Studies acted locally but thought and continue to think globally. The connection between the Third and First Worlds is constant via migration and diaspora. Given the greater movement of peoples around the globe in recent decades, we are just beginning to recognize that where people live and work—their geographical location—affects their outlook along with demography, perhaps even more so.

Demography and Geography

Demographic change occurs over decades and cohorts. Public policies and natural or man-made disasters or events contribute to these changes. For example, China's 1979 policy of "One child per family" was created to slow down overpopulation. By 2015, however, it was being phased out, as the policy contributed to a greater proportion of men than women, causing a sex ratio imbalance, a larger dependent aging population, and a decreasing younger productive labor force population. In addition, the 2008 Sichuan province earthquake whereby almost 70,000 people were killed precipitated an exception to the "One child policy" for parents who had lost children in the earthquake.

A US example is the effects of the 1965 Immigration Act, which removed restrictions on various national origin quotas and gave preference to family reunification, domestic labor force needs, and refugee/humanitarian needs. The last category was very much at play at the end of the American war in Southeast Asia. The population change was not readily seen until the 1980 Census. The shift was at first gradual. It was first occurred among the Asian American population with the entry of refugees from the American war in Southeast Asia. With the April 30, 1975 fall of Saigon, 131,000 persons from South Vietnam, Laos and Cambodia were evacuated and resettled as refugees in the US. The 1975 Refugee Resettlement Act further increased numbers in the following years. Furthermore, as in all wars, the birth of children of military men and the women where wars were fought needed to be addressed. In 1982, the Amerasian Immigration Act prioritized entry to the US for children fathered by US citizens from various Asian countries including Korea, Laos, Cambodia, Vietnam and Thailand. In 1989, the Amerasian Homecoming Act was implemented, including preferential immigration status to these children's families—including mother, spouse, child, and next of kin. The 1980 Census enumerated about 231,000 persons in the Vietnamese Immigrant (foreign born) population. By 2014 this had increased to 1,292,000.

Another example is the growth of the Filipino population in the US. This growth was not based on refugee status but other factors. After the Philippine Revolution against Spain, the US fought the Filipino people in order to seize the Philippines at beginning of the twentieth century and make it part of its overseas colonial empire, which included Hawaii and Puerto Rico. In addition to owning the natural resources of the Philippines, the human capital of Filipinos was used in creating the 20th century American economy. In the early 20th century, Filipinos along with Japanese and Chinese workers, were recruited by American companies as agricultural laborers in Hawaii and California. During most of the

20th century, Filipinos were recruited by the US as military personnel, predominantly in the Navy and as medical, health, administrative, and other professionals. Coupled with the 1965 immigration priority for family reunification, Filipino populations were able to increase dramatically. The 1960 Census indicated a Filipino immigrant population of about 105,000. By the 1980 Census it was closer to 500,000, and by the 2010 Census, it was closer to 2,000,000. This does not include US-born children of prior generations since the early 1900s. Though viewed as a black/white society as late as the 1970 Census, the 1980 Census documented that red, brown and yellow populations were coloring this dichotomy.

Demographic characteristics are the features of a human population and are not just race, sex, and age. Also included are cohort, foreign or native birth, rural or urban residence, citizenship, and migration/mobility. As the statistical and systematic study of populations, demography allows greater recognition, understanding, and inclusion of various groups via censuses, surveys, and administrative records. Demographic data for federal and other public policies are used to assess whether federal resources serve the needs of American citizens and residents. Demographic data area also used for other purposes, such as targeted marketing to serve the wants of consumers.

The Color Line

The student movements and colonial revolutions of the 1950s and 1960s publicized Third World nations and peoples in the US and abroad, making us cognizant of geography. Yet, it is the color line, the shade of skin color that is the direct, physical manifestation separating privileged whites and the rest of mankind around the world. The first Black Harvard PhD sociologist, W.E.B. DuBois, concluded that, "The problem of the twentieth century is the problem of the color-line." Born a free Black person to property owners in Great Barrington, Massachusetts, DuBois also traveled to the Mid-Atlantic and South, attending and teaching at historically Black colleges. He went abroad, undertaking graduate work at the University of Berlin and was traveled across Europe. While participating in the first Pan-African Conference in London in 1900, he made his observation of the color line. DuBois was also involved with the National Association for the Advancement of Colored People (NAACP). With its 1909 founding, the NAACP was a pioneer institution formally recognizing people of color. The color line was not just a demographic characteristic. It was accompanied by the geographic contours of place and mobility.

As noted earlier, the SF State student-led strike and establishment of ethnic studies can be viewed as part of the Civil Rights Movement, which was initially southern, black/white, and primarily rural after World War II. The second stage was northern, urban, and primarily black/white, as exemplified by the 1966 Chicago Freedom Movement, whose goal was to end slums in the cities. Reverend Dr. King noted that the hostility of White mobs to Black civil rights issues in Chicago was greater than he had experienced in the South. The third stage of the growing civil rights movement was western and made up of the Golden Children of rural and urban California.

While many of the white students and students of color at SF State were local, they also included persons who had migrated to California, such as members of the Negro Students Association and Black Student Union. Of equal interest were the administrators of color who supported the students. For example, Joseph White, a pioneer in the field of Black psychology who went on to be a founder of the Association of Black Psychologists, was a thirty-something dean of Undergraduate Studies during the strike. He grew up in Minnesota and attended SF State for his bachelor and master's degrees. His PhD was from Michigan State University. He noted that in an overwhelmingly white Midwest, he didn't face overt discrimination. It was when looking for housing as a professor at California State University, Long Beach State that he encountered racism. Professor White left SF State and went on to build a reputation on cross-cultural psychology, challenging the arrogance of Eurocentric psychology as the discipline's norm.[2]

Reginald Major was the first director of the Educational Opportunity

---

2 Anna M. Phillips, "Joseph White, pioneering black psychologist who mentored students at U.C. Irvine dies at 84," *Los Angeles Times*, December 1, 2017, https://fortmason.org/event/sanctuary/.

Program during the strike. A journalist and author, he grew up in Harlem and attended the University of Chicago. For Bay Area and California students like me coming from ethnic and racial neighborhoods, meeting administrators and faculty of color from the Midwest and East Coast was new and refreshing. What was even more unusual was that administrators and faculty of color from elite universities east of the Mississippi River were interested in talking to and recruiting the activists at San Francisco State.

Go East, Young Women and Men

SF State did not introduce Black Studies/ethnic studies courses via the strike. Such courses had already existed separately for several years. SF State was following the momentum of organic efforts such as in the local community colleges, the campus' own Experimental College, and scattered courses on other campuses and selected communities. It was part of something bigger than itself. What SF State uniquely did was to institutionalize disparate efforts across various racial/ethnic groups and define them as a Third World College, with various departments and Full Time Equivalent resources. It offered an institutional alternative to Eurocentric higher education. Ending the four-month strike and establishing ethnic studies at SF State was accomplished by collaboration and negotiation among students, faculty administration, staff, community organizations, organized labor, businesses, government representatives, and institutions of faith. This is the only campus strike and ethnic studies fight that had all of these parties involved. Across the nation, to avoid more explosive campuses from West to East and from San Francisco State to Cornell, universities, including elite ones, offered ethnic studies courses and hired people of color to administer and teach them. Just as the urban riots of the 1960s precipitated the rise of Black journalists and radio and television reporters, the campus protests served as catalyst for people of color into the academy.

After graduation with undergraduate degrees, several strike leaders and activists were invited to meet with recruiters for graduate and professional schools such as Cornell, Columbia, Brown and the University of Chicago. We were also invited to meet with California recruiters from Stanford, UCSF, UCLA, and UC Berkeley. We were told that if we were going to be agents of change, they would prefer for us to make changes within the system; to be part of the system. Of course, some students and faculty debated that these recruitment efforts were cooptation. Many of our parents, on the other hand, thought it was an opportunity to welcome and seize. It was what pioneer Black attorney Florynce Kennedy called seizing the small window of opportunity before it closes again. A sizable number of us accepted invitations and became part of the historic cohort of the first white women and people of color in our families to go to graduate and professional schools and enter professions and industries from which our parents and grandparents had been systematically excluded.

In the footsteps of our parents and ancestors we continued the great migration and spreading of diaspora. They moved from village to town; from town to city; from one country to another, crossing rivers and oceans. As immigrants or refugees, they left their countries of origin. As citizens they moved from segregated/designated sections of the United States. By entering advanced and elite institutions of education and employment, we, their children, were going to be global citizens moving beyond a Eurocentric geography and demography.

As Henry Wu poignantly noted during his research as a graduate student, "Through those long hours on America's roads, I realized that coming to know something is often a physical as well as an intellectual movement, that coming to knowledge is not something that occurs only in a study room or a research lab somewhere in a university; sometimes it is an act strewn across a landscape of ignorance. It is a leaving of some familiar place in order to trace a series of journeys into the unknown.[3]

This recruitment of non-traditional students was not necessarily new, nor limited to white women and people of color. In the 1960s, for example, the University of Chicago created a similar program for young scholars in rural areas, starting with six Midwestern states called the Small School Talent Search, informally labeled GRITS (Grass Roots

---

3   Henry Yu, *Thinking Orientals: Migration, Contact and Exoticism in Modern America* (New York: Oxford University Press, 2001), v.

Talent Search).[4] The program was born of necessity when enrollment of traditional (privileged white male) undergraduate students went down by 50 percent in the College. The high school seniors that were recruited were good students who set their goals on state schools or local colleges, not an elite private university. As these students did not generally meet the more rigorous academic and urbane requirements, there were cultural and expectations gaps. Fifty years later, one student summarized the most consistent criticism of the program as, "They pretty much just said welcome, we're glad you're here, and threw me into the deep end."[5] Little was offered to help with deficiencies or bridge the cultural chasm between small towns and an urban community of scholars. Some students were able to adjust and even do well, while others did not. For the SF State 1968–69 strikers and activists, new cultures produced results that were equally mixed. At the 40th anniversary commemoration of the strike, various alumni shared their experiences.

Vern E. Smith was an active member of the BSU during the strike, which he described as scary and exhilarating. Like other interviewees, he reaffirmed that there were so many social and political changes during this period that one had to take a stand and get involved, especially as they saw the strike expand. Strikers could draw strength from one other.[6] He graduated from S.F. State in 1969. That summer he attended the Summer Program for Minority Journalists at Columbia University Graduate School of Journalism. He became a correspondent for *Newsweek* and was assigned to the Detroit, MI and Atlanta, GA bureaus. In 1997, Smith was named *Newsweek* National Correspondent. He closed his interview by thanking the students for an expanded worldview facilitated by the College of Ethnic Studies.

As one of the SF State strike leaders featured in *Agents of Change*, Ramona Tascoe took her strike activism to medical school at the University of California, San Francisco and became a practicing physician

---

4 Tom Heberlein, "No Small Talent," *University of Chicago Magazine*, Winter 2017, 30-33.
5 Ibid., 33.
6 "Don Smothers and Vern Smith Interview," SFSU COES, 10:50, https://diva.sfsu.edu/bundles/218204.

in the Bay Area. Her decades of experience in public health took her to the East Coast and around the world. This experience included work on policy issues with the Office of Research on Women's Health in the National Institutes of Health. Internationally, Dr. Tascoe contributed to addressing public health, sustainable development, and disaster response/recovery issues in East Africa, India, Sri Lanka, and Haiti.

Danny Glover graduated from George Washington High School. After SF State, he became a community development administrator for the city of San Francisco and attended the Black Actors' Workshop of the American Conservatory Theater. Instead of moving east, he moved south to Los Angeles to study film, stage, and television. In 1985, along with Oprah Winfrey and Whoopi Goldberg, he made his film debut in *The Color Purple*, Alice Walker's Pulitzer Prize novel directed by Steven Spielberg. Today Glover is an internationally recognized actor, film director, and political activist.

The Midwest Connection

Many strikers and activists stayed in the Bay Area to continue their off- and on-campus community organizing and academic, family, and labor force activities. A sizable number left the comfort zone of the Bay Area to go south to UCLA, across the country, across the Atlantic, the Pacific, and the Rio Grande. Some Boomer graduates who moved east also made a Midwest connection. As part of my community work after graduating from SF State in 1970, I served on the community advisory committee for San Francisco General Hospital. There I met Dr. David Sanchez, a Latino sociologist at UCSF and fellow advisory committee member. He suggested I consider going beyond my comfort zone and applying to the University of Chicago. For an orientation, he graciously introduced me to his brother who, with a handful of Latinos, was studying there. I was also recruited by UCLA but was encouraged to head for the University of Chicago by another sociologist, Lucie Cheng Hirata, the first permanent director of the UCLA Asian American Studies Center.

Over time, I discovered that the University of Chicago was often a stopping place for students of color at some point in their academic careers. In particular, the university prided itself on admissions and graduation of

Black students. "Between 1870 and 1940, 45 African American students were granted PhDs, more than at any other institution in the nation. In the first decade of the 20th century alone, nine African Americans earned undergraduate degrees, while five more earned graduate degrees. . . . today, the list of graduates reads like a Who's Who of African American intellectuals in the post-Reconstruction era: Monroe Nathan Work, Carter G. Woodson, Benjamin Mays, Katherine Dunham, and Vivian Harsh, to name a few. In the last years of the 20th century, a new wave of faculty luminaries kept that tradition alive, including E. Franklin Frazier, John Hope Franklin, William Julius Wilson, and Barack Obama."[7] In the first half of the 20th century, the Chicago School of Sociology was well known for its research on the urban environment and race. An influential figure was Robert Park, whose theories of race, including dominant and subordinate peoples and spatial segregation, had been influenced in the urban setting as a Chicago newspaper reporter, in the South as a visiting professor at Fisk University, and on the West Coast as research director for the Race Relations Survey of the Pacific Coast during the Asian Exclusion Act of 1924. The idea of doing primary fieldwork and gathering data to inform theory—conducting applied research—was inherent to the school. But their fieldwork required looking at the urban setting as a laboratory from which they were the detached, objective outsider. Furthermore, the populations being studied were viewed as problems and given labels like juvenile delinquents and aliens, their transgression the failure to assimilate to the dominant culture.

Founded in 1890 with funding from John D. Rockefeller, Marshall Field, and the American Baptist Education Society, the purpose of the University of Chicago was "a commitment to rigorous academics for people of all backgrounds, including "opportunities for all departments of higher education to persons of both sexes on equal terms."[8] When elite universities such as Harvard, Yale and Princeton did not allow women students until the 1970s, a few including Chicago, Stanford and

---

7   Deva Woodly, "How UChicago became a hub for Black intellectuals," https://www.uchicago.edu/features/20090119_mlk/.
8   "The University of Chicago: The Early Years," *University of Chicago*, https://www.uchicago.edu/about/history/.

Columbia, allowed a very few women.

Given this background, it was not so unusual that Nathan Hare and Reginald Major were Chicago alumni. In terms of gender, Patsy Takemoto Mink attended the University of Chicago Law School, receiving her Juris Doctorate in 1951. She was the first woman elected to Congress from the state of Hawaii. In 1972, she became the first Asian American to seek the presidential nomination of the Democratic Party, where she stood in the Oregon primary as an anti-war candidate. She was a primary sponsor of Title IX of the federal Education Amendments of 1972, which opened up doors in higher education for girls and young women, including sports. Just before her death in September 2002, Mrs. Mink addressed a welcoming luncheon of university students serving as summer interns in the capital sponsored by the University of Chicago D.C Alumni Club. She noted that her initial goal was to be a physician but had been turned down by medical schools because she was a woman. At Chicago, she was accepted as a law student but placed in a foreign student dorm and assigned to an English language class. While people of color and white women had greater access at Chicago than at elite other universities, their numbers were quite modest, even in the 1970s.

While looking at UCLA's graduate program, I was surprised to learn from trailblazer Lucie Cheng Hirata that she had received her master's degree in library science at Chicago. Subsequently, I was told by Penelope Flores, education professor emeritus, San Francisco State, that she had received her PhD in comparative and international education from Chicago. Wherever I turned, there seemed to be this Midwest connection. Malcolm Collier, along with his wife, Irene Dea Collier, was instrumental in developing Asian American Studies/Chinese American Studies at SF State and gave me letters of introduction to his uncle and aunt who were professors at Chicago. His own father, John Collier, Jr., known for pioneering visual anthropology and visual sociology, especially in his study of American Indians, was a professor of education and anthropology at SF State. His grandfather, John Collier, Sr., was a sociologist and head of the Bureau of Indian Affairs during President Franklin Roosevelt's New Deal.

As a student of ethnic studies, especially Asian American Studies, I and other students of color were intrigued by our shared connection with the University of Chicago, which continued throughout our careers, within and outside of academia. The Chicago connection was an interesting observation for me during my career as a federal demographer based in Washington, DC. Colleagues at the US Commission on Civil Rights, Pattie Tom and Professor Esther Chow, had also graduated from the Chicago School. Other students of color, including Nampeo McKenney, chief architect for racial and ethnic statistics at the US Census Bureau and her assistant, Claudette Bennett, had also been taught by Chicago sociology/demography professors.

The Chicago connection came to the forefront when Ellen Wu, history professor and director of Asia American Studies at Indiana University, interviewed me in 2017 for her book, which includes the historical evolution of Asian Americans as an official minority group in the 1960s and 1970s.[9] Ellen introduced me to Henry Yu's provocative and insightful book, *Thinking Orientals: Migration, Contact, and Exoticism in Modern America*.[10] Henry's book is "an attempt to answer why it is that an Asian American in the United States, no matter how long and for how many generations he or she might have been here, will still be regularly asked, 'Where are you from?'" His book first notes how self-appointed white experts and reformers in the context of the birth of the social sciences and the popularity of the eugenics movement defined Orientals as being exotic and from distant lands and hence being un-American, while defining themselves as White and American. Second, although a few Asians and Asian Americans were in universities, "Asian Americans, like African Americans and other intellectuals of color in the United States, did not (and in many ways still do not) have the range of possibilities that white scholars enjoyed."[11] Henry goes on to conclude, "The white Protestant men who came to understand Orientals in the early twentieth century had first say in defining the meaning of Orientals in America. The Chinese Americans and Japanese Americans who came to sociology in the twentieth century said and did a great number of things, but they

---

9   Ellen Dionne Wu, personal communication with author, May 19, 2016.
10   Henry Yu, *Thinking Orientals* (Oxford: Oxford University Press, 2002).
11   Ibid., vii.

performed on a stage that was mostly not of their making." [12]

While the University of Chicago provided access to students of color, even noting them as intellectuals, their self-determination and separate intellectual traditions were not necessarily acknowledged nor encouraged. Students of color, like white women, were expected to fit the "Chicago mold," to assimilate. This was a dilemma as they were not white males of the dominant group.

In 1903 in *The Souls of Black Folks*, W.E.B. Dubois, an icon and Black intellectual not of the Chicago School, described this psychological conflict by minority groups as "double consciousness." Due to their subordinate position in society, people of color (and white women) were being measured by a standard they could never attain. They were judged by an outsider. Interestingly, the University of Chicago also produced white male scholars in the 1950s and 1960s who had a similar take on being able to have a double role or double understanding of outsider and insider. One was Howard Becker who wrote *Outsiders: Studies in Sociology of Deviance* and the other Erving Goffman, who wrote *Presentation of Self in Everyday Life*. Becker utilized the participation observer method as a jazz musician who explored the worlds of marijuana users and musicians who were both considered outsiders or labeled as members of deviant cultures. Goffman posed as an assistant athletic director in his study of mental hospitals in order to observe life in mental institutions unobtrusively. In his various research areas, Goffman observed that individuals usually chose how to present themselves to others depending on the accepted behavior for a given social situation. For Asian Americans and other people of color, how they saw themselves was not necessarily how the dominant group saw them. Oftentimes they were judged not just as inferior and unequal but irrelevant, marginal, exotic, and invisible. Asian American academics during this period were the first post-World War II PhDs, and getting tenured positions was a challenge despite their degrees. For example, S.I. Hayakawa, a Canadian American, received his PhD from the University of Wisconsin in 1935, but in the early 1950s he was a part-time lecturer at the University of Chicago. In 1955, he moved west to accept a professorship at San Francisco State.

---

12 Ibid., vii.

The idea of "Asian Americans" is a late 20th century concept and term arising from the student movement of the 1960s that was codified in federal statistical policies of the 1970s, so that the identity was not only one of self-determination but also self-identification in the federal Decennial Census of Population and Housing. Before then, persons of Asian ancestry were defined as "Oriental." In the media, they were usually Japanese and Chinese since they were the largest groups before the 1965 Immigration Act amendments. At the University of Chicago, with the Oriental Institute founded in 1919, "Oriental" initially referred to ancient Near Eastern civilizations. With the increase of Asians in Hawaii and the West Coast, primarily as laborers recruited by American companies for the transcontinental railroad and agricultural industries, the term used for Japanese and Chinese was pejorative, as in "the Oriental problem." The issue was that they could not be assimilated. In 1966 in a *New York Times* article, sociologist William Petersen labeled Japanese Americans as 'the model minority' distinct from Black and brown minorities. Other Asian Americans were given or even adopted this description. In 2018, a University of Chicago annual fundraising campaign request featured an Asian American assistant professor female social scientist promoting funding for research that integrates social science, health science, and population science. There is no mention of conducting research for the public good or serving communities in need.

Californians and Others Shift East

The American dilemma of the "Oriental problem", "the Negro problem," "the Mexican problem," and the "Indian problem" was effectively challenged by communities of color in the latter half of the 20th century. With "Black Power" emanating from southern states and urban centers of the north and "Red Power," "Brown Power" and "Yellow Power" reverberating West of the Mississippi, demographic and geographic changes headed towards Washington. In the 1960s, with the presidencies of Lyndon Johnson representing Texas and the Southwest and Richard Nixon representing California and the West, great shifts occurred politically, geographically, and demographically. Politically, the Republican Party was no longer the party of Abraham Lincoln, civil rights, and the

New England/Boston Brahmins. The southern Democrats became Republican and the New England Rockefeller/Elliott Richardson/Bush Republicans diminished. Geographically, power east of the Mississippi began to give way to west of the Mississippi. Demographically, population growth shifted west where Asians, Latinos, American Indians, Alaskan Natives and Pacific Islanders were concentrated. Hawaii and Alaska had recently become states.

Presidents Johnson and Nixon grew up aware of non-white folks—Mexicans, American Indians, Black people, Filipinos, Chinese, Japanese, and Mestizos. They brought this familiarity with non-white sensibility and experience with them to DC along with their West Coast cabinet members. For the Department of Health Education and Welfare (DHEW), I think of Bob Finch and Caspar Weinberger. Other cabinet secretaries like George Schultz developed a western mentality. These leaders wanted to avoid more confrontations like the summer urban riots and college campus uprisings of the late 1960s. It behooved them to consider and fund various programs—affirmative action and equal employment/education programs aimed at minority communities and to recruit traditionally-excluded people of color to elite universities and government work.

In the 1970s, young people fresh out of college went to Washington, DC and met each other across color, race, and geographic identities. With affirmative action paving the way, federal programs created by Presidents John Kennedy and Lyndon Johnson in the 1960s—from the Peace Corps to the Office of Economic Opportunity—provided these idealistic youth with occupations from which they could serve their communities.

In 1973, I was fresh out of graduate school from the University of Chicago and a new bride in Washington, DC applying for a federal position. I moved from a California of Golden Children to a Midwest of Black and whites but more precisely ethnic whites of Irish, Italian, Polish, and German descent. I then moved again, not just east but also south of the Mason-Dixon Line to the DC suburbs. In 1973, Black people comprised the majority in the nation's capital while whites continued fleeing to the suburbs. The few Asians or Hispanics there were associated with the foreign embassies, the World Bank, the International Monetary Fund and other international organizations. The even fewer American Indians were associated with the Bureau of Indian Affairs of the US Department of the Interior or the Indian Health Service in the Public Health Service of the US Department of Health, Education and Welfare. The federal government was primarily represented in the DC area by white people from east of the Mississippi and Black people from the south. There were also non-profit organizations proliferating from direct community services to policy analysis, again with top positions filled by whites.

With the election of Richard Nixon as president in 1968 and 1972, the presence of politicians and their staffs from California and other western states (including the newest states of Alaska and Hawaii) began to be visible in the nation's capital. In addition, women and people of color newly graduated from professional and graduate schools took their next steps in affirmative action by entering professions from which they were traditionally excluded, namely mid-level and senior level positions, in private and public institutions, including the federal government. For positions in the latter, the first step was to pass the civil service exam at a very high level, usually at 100%. Then one was ranked with other applicants within a given occupation. The idea was to be in a specialized category with few competitors. At that point, "Social Science Analyst" was a relatively new and specialized occupation. When candidates were of equal merit, other factors could be considered such as underrepresentation. I figured as a minority woman I was a two'fer, a shoo-in. I later found out that I was selected not due to those factors but because Californians were underrepresented in the federal workforce.

Again, I had the feeling of being in the right place at the right time. As I researched the dynamics of the resolution of the SF State strike in Sacramento for this book, I learned that the Nixon cabinet was full of men, like him, from California, including Caspar Weinberger and Robert Finch, who was Ronald Reagan's Lieutenant Governor. Both Finch and Weinberger served as secretaries of the Department of Health, Education, and Welfare. These men were aware of this growing electorate. The increasing numbers of people of color in California and the increasing student activism in the University of California and California State University systems demanded state and federal responses. The federal governmental response at the elementary and secondary education levels occurred earlier in 1965 with passage of Title I of the Elementary and Secondary Education Act. This law was passed to improve the academic achievement of disadvantaged children including children in the nation's highest poverty schools, limited English proficient children, migrant children, children with disabilities, Indian children, and neglected or delinquent children. It sought to close the achievement gap between minority and non-minority students. This was the era of means-tested programs, which required demographic and other data to qualify program beneficiaries. In 1969, President Nixon established the Cabinet Committee on Opportunities for Spanish Speaking People. In 1970, he issued a Sixteen-Point Federal Employment Program to increase Hispanic representation in the federal workforce

For college graduates of color, as well as their white counterparts, serving the community via public service made sense. One of the first federal employees who welcomed me to Washington, DC was Franklin Chow from San Francisco Chinatown. He had graduated several years earlier from San Francisco State, served in the Air Force, and participated with several Bay Area residents in the Civil Rights Movement Freedom Rides. He served in the Equal Employment Opportunity Commission. Another was Phil Chin, who had also been on strike at SF State and was an analyst in the Office of Asian American Affairs in the Office of Special Concerns, Office of the Secretary at DHEW. Franklin, Phil, other Asian Americans from the West Coast, and I met young Latinos from the Southwest and Black people from the South and Midwest who also came to the nation's capital to begin their careers at DHEW and other federal agencies such as the US Commission on Civil Rights, the Equal Employment Opportunity Commission, the US Census Bureau, and the Smithsonian Institution. One of the first persons I met in DC was Jimmy Garrett, who had left the Bay Area along with John Summerskill in 1968. Jimmy was at the Institute for Policy Studies conducting research on Third World people in the US and abroad.

The Office of Education, Department of Health, Education, and Welfare

In my view, the first agency in the federal government that became attuned to the shifting demographics of the Bay Area and California was the Office of Education, then a part of DHEW. The Office housed the National Center for Education Statistics, which, among other things, collected information on students via school districts. In order to know the demography of a geographic area twenty years forward, one can look at who is being born today and the make-up of kindergarteners and first graders.

Title I allowed collection of such data. Other federal agencies also collected demographic and beneficiary information in order to evaluate the effectiveness of federal programs, monitor the enforcement of civil rights statutes and services, and track distribution of federal funds. The Federal Interagency Committee on Education (FICE) was composed of federal departments with educational programs. Given changing demographics and geographical mobility, FICE was tasked with developing standardized racial and ethnic categories for use by the government. In preparing the federal statistical policy directive governing racial and ethnic categories, FICE identified American Indian or Alaskan Native, Asian or Pacific Islander, Black/Negro, Caucasian/White, and Hispanic.[13] Except for Caucasian/White, these categories matched the populations in SF State's College of Ethnic Studies. The development of formal racial categories for the federal statistical system were largely based on the SF State categories. The members of the Ad Hoc Committee on Racial and Ethnic Definitions of the Federal Interagency Committee on Education included statisticians, demographers, civil rights attorneys, and program managers. They were both white and people of color, men and women. They represented a range of agencies from the Census Bureau to the Bureau of Labor Statistics, the Bureau of Indian Affairs, the Office of Management and Budget, the US Army, the

---

13   Federal Interagency Committee on Education, Washington, DC, "Report of the Ad Hoc Committee on Racial and Ethnic Definitions of the Federal Interagency Committee on Education, April 1975," *ERIC*, https://files.eric. ed.gov/fulltext/ED121636.pdf.

Equal Employment Opportunity Commission, and the Department of Health, Education, and Welfare. Within DHEW there were staff from the Office for Civil Rights, the Office of Asian American Affairs and Office for Spanish Surnamed Americans.[14]

The Office of Special Concerns, US Department of Health, Education and Welfare

When Phil Chin initially went to work at DHEW in 1972, the Secretary was Elliott Richardson, a progressive Brahmin Republican (a radical moderate in his own words). Within the Office of the Secretary a unit was created in 1970 called the Office of Special Concerns. Under this umbrella were the Women's Action Program, the Office of American Indian Affairs, the Office of Asian American Affairs, the Office of Black American Affairs, and the Office for Spanish Surnamed Americans. The DHEW racial and ethnic offices mirrored the racial and ethnic departments of the then School of Ethnic Studies at SF State. Staff included new college graduates of young Black and Asian Americans from California and Mexican Americans from the Southwest. Under Secretary Richardson, in addition to the Office of Special Concerns, there were other new innovative programs including Upward Mobility, which allowed DHEW employees from populations traditionally excluded from higher education—that is, racial/ethnic minorities and women—to go to college while being paid their salaries, with DHEW covering tuition and expenses. This was evocative of SF State's earlier Educational Opportunity and Upward Bound Programs. Another was a Prisoner Workforce Re-entry Program where folks who had served their sentences were placed in federal jobs. One of my sociology professors at SF State in 1969, John Irwin, also an ex-prisoner, pioneered a similar, very successful, award-winning program, Project Rebound, which continues today. Also, the first study of American farmworkers, many migrant workers, was initiated in the Office of Special Concerns under Secretary Richardson.

---

14   Juanita Tamayo Lott, "Policy Purposes of Race and Ethnicity: An Assessment of Federal Racial and Ethnic Categories," *Ethnicity & Disease*, vol. 3 no. 3, (Summer 1993): 221-228.

By the time I got to the Office of Asian American Affairs (OAAA) in 1973, Elliott Richardson had left DHEW, moved on to become Secretary of Defense, and then became Attorney General at the Department of Justice. Elliott Richardson made history by refusing to obey President Nixon's order to fire Watergate special prosecutor Archibald Cox. He chose to resign instead that year. Caspar Weinberger replaced him at DHEW. In the Office of Asian American Affairs, Phil and I worked with director Toyo Biddle and consultant Canta Pian, who had been on strike at UC Berkeley against the Vietnam War and for Ethnic studies. Canta taught one of the first Asian American Studies classes at Cal. Phil co-founded the Asian and Pacific American Federal Employee Caucus (APAFEC) with Art Bigornia, who was one of the first Asian American Social Security Administration program managers and who hailed from Vallejo, CA. APAFEC worked with BIG (Blacks in Government) and Hispanic employee groups. At OAAA, several of our summer interns throughout the 1970s came from Cal in the Capital, a University of California, Berkeley program. These students had taken Asian American or other ethnic studies courses at the UC, SF State, or other CSU campuses. Some, such as UC Santa Cruz professor Dana Takagi and Hawaii attorney Joyce Matsumori went on to become the first cohort of ethnic studies professionals to serve their local communities after having gone east to the nation's capital. Throughout my four-decade Washington, DC career in the federal government and as inside-the-beltway consultant, I've met Asian American and non-Asian American folks early in their career, looking for jobs, who say that an ethnic studies course or two focused them to think about community service at a non-profit organization or in the local, state or federal government.

An early dilemma for the DHEW and the federal government generally was that the racial/ethnic minorities represented by the Office of Special Concerns were primarily in the South, Southwest and West Coast while in Washington, DC federal government professionals were mainly white males from East and Mid-Atlantic states. Black people mainly from the South, and other minorities were mostly in non-professional slots. Over time, recruitment of historically underrepresented groups to federal service has improved. Compared to the private sector, the public sector has an increased proportion of people of color in the workforce.

In the 1970s the nation's capital became more aware of people of color with the end of the war in Southeast Asia. While direct US military involvement ended in summer 1973, the official ending of the war was April 1975 with the fall of Saigon to the North Vietnamese. The Office of Asian American Affairs worked with the relatively new Office of Refugee Resettlement, detailing Dr. Freda Cheung of the National Institute of Mental Health and Dr. Jonathan Chang of the Office of Education, to review programs and services to Vietnamese, Hmong, Laotian, and Cambodian refugees. Historically, prior federal refugee resettlement was primarily directed to European refugees who were cared for by mainline Protestant social service agencies east of the Mississippi. The Southeast Asian refugee resettlement crisis necessitated the involvement of Asian American community organizations and non-profits west of the Mississippi to provide more culturally relevant services to these new Americans. Many of these organizations were direct creations of the community service components of Asian American Studies/Ethnic Studies at San Francisco State and other campuses. The federal government was responsible not just for providing services to the refugees but for keeping track of its newest residents to ensure they were given the assistance due them. DHEW was unable to do this on its own. It required the services of the federal statistical system via survey data, evaluation studies, and the Decennial Census of Population and Housing.

The 1980 Census Racial and Ethnic Advisory Committees, Census Bureau

The 1975 FICE Report, noted above, was delivered to the Office of Management and Budget (OMB) which primarily relied on it in issuing OMB Statistical Policy Directive 15: Race and Ethnic Standards for Federal Statistics and Administrative Reporting, 1977.[15] As the linchpin of the federal statistical system, the US Census Bureau adhered to this

---

15   Barry Edmonston, Joshua Goldstein, Juanita Tamayo Lott eds., *Spotlight on Heterogeneity: the Federal Standards for Racial and Ethnic Classification*, (Washington, D.C.: National Academy Press, 1996), Appendix B.

statistical policy directive in the planning, conduct, evaluation, and analysis of 1980 Decennial Census of Population and Housing. The major racial and ethnic categories for the 1980 Census mirrored the population groups of SF State College of Ethnic Studies.

Given its mandate to count all the American people, to acknowledge that the United States had moved beyond the designations of black and white and the urgent need to identify the Southeast Asian populations, the US Census Bureau created several racial and ethnic advisory committees for the 1980 Census. Since the first census in 1790 and through the decades, the Census Bureau has relied on a variety of advisors. In the 20th century, advisory committees included members from academia, business and professional associations such as the American Statistical Association, the American Marketing Association, the Population Association of America, and the American Economic Association.

The first racial and ethnic Census Bureau advisory committees were established under Vincent Barabba, who has the distinction of serving twice as Census Bureau director under one Democratic and two Republican presidents, from 1973–1976 and then 1979–1981. A Californian, Mr. Barabba is internationally known for his innovative market research and opinion polling over five decades. His 2017 book, *Wise Decision Making through the Use of Systemic Knowledge and Imagination*, provides examples of looking at systems not through individual parts but through the interaction of the parts. I believe that is how he viewed the racial and ethnic advisory committees and their members, as well as bureau staff —dynamic, interacting, interconnected parts of the system called the decennial census.

An excerpt from Mr. Barabba's Oral History interview with Census Bureau staff provides a sample of the relevance and contributions of the racial and ethnic minority advisory committees.

"In my first term, we had the first minority committee meetings outside of the Bureau. They said, "You guys have got to demonstrate that you're serious," so we went to Chicago, and had first the Black Committee [session there]. We went some place on the south side of Chicago; it was really tough, but it was one of the best meetings I attended. I'm sitting up on a dais with Lonnie [Abdul Alim] Shabazz from the Moslems, Althea Simmons, George Riddick from Operation PUSH. Anyway, it was one of the most rewarding experiences I've ever been through, because I did not have to answer the questions. One lady got up and said, "If you are really serious about counting, then why are you asking all these personal questions [in the census]?" I'm about ready to respond when this Black legislator gets up in the middle of the room. He said, 'The reason they ask those questions is that they are important. I passed legislation that demonstrated that a telephone was an essential instrument in every home so that people could communicate, and it should be taken off their listed assets, as well as a television set. I was able to use Bureau statistics that say that a telephone is not a luxury item for a family to have, it's a form of communication. If I had not had the Bureau statistics, I couldn't have built it into my legislation.' That was a lot more impartial than anything I would have said.

"Then the next day, we went to the Hispanic Advisory Committee, in another part of Chicago, and they really had set us up. They had this big group come in and picket: They wanted us to use the city of Chicago as the test area for the 1980 census. Well, that [would be] a pretty big test. I was trying to explain to them why [this would not be] feasible, but they didn't [want to] hear about it, so we finally closed the meeting off. While we were getting on the bus back to the hotel, we noticed that Meyer Zitter had taken one of the signs that said 'Chicago for a test site' and changed it to 'Chicago for an atomic test site.' We all had a good laugh. I would say that it was interesting, when you think about all the lawsuits that we have, that the only time a minority organization showed up in the suits that went through was sometimes as a friend of the court, or as added to a municipal lawsuit, but I don't think any of the minority communities instituted a suit.

"Let me put it this way: If you would have listed all of the people that were going to line up and have lawsuits against the Bureau in 1980, you would have had all of the minority communities at the front of the list. Now, where it broke down was with the municipal leaders, the elected officials. But I would say that in many ways the minority people were really sophisticated. They had a lot to say about who was working on the census. If we had a census tract [with errors in the data] showing up, we fixed it while they were there. They were sworn in as Bureau agents during the test in Austin [Travis County, TX, 1976], and they came back and reported about what they learned once they knew that we weren't hiding anything. Then they knew we were doing a pretty thorough job, so you had a strong leadership community. I think most of them were, I'd say, very professional in how they handled themselves. They would yell and scream at you. Vilma Martinez [member of the 1980 Hispanic Advisory Committee from the Mexican American Defense and Education Fund], God bless her, I mean when you got through that meeting, you knew you had been through a meeting, but on the other hand, you could call her up and say, "This group over there is about to take us to court for the wrong reason," and she would go explain to them. She would do it very quietly. She had her own political environment to maintain, but they did a lot of quiet diplomacy for us.

"More importantly, and that was their main objective, they really helped us in the outreach program to demonstrate the value of the census to those communities, so the communities themselves at the local level would have an active program of participation. That is why we had the census use activity early, in the latter part of the 1970's, so people would know what to do with the 1980 data when they got to the data. They knew what the limitations were. They would say [about the 1970 data], 'That is wrong,' so you say, 'Well, here is how you fix it in 1980: you make sure you get counted.' That part, I think, all worked out very well. Some of my colleagues say it was very helpful, but it was very painful. On balance, if I had to list the very helpful things in the 1980 census, that would be one."[16]

The ability to obtain a complete census in part depended on ensuring active support of persons to be counted. In the 1980 census this support occurred via recruitment of indigenous staffs, outreach to various minority constituencies, and advice on questionnaire wording (especially race and ethnicity items) and data products. Census Bureau staff stressed the use of data to improve people's lives. In 1976, charters were drawn for three Census Advisory Committees—Asian and Pacific Islander, Black, and Hispanic. At that time, American Indian and Alaskan Native communities decided not to have a formal advisory body. Formal names were the Census Advisory Committee on Asian and Pacific Islander Americans Populations for the 1980 Census, Census Advisory Committee on the Black Population for the 1980 Census, and Census Advisory Committee on the Spanish Origin Populations for the 1980 Census.

In addition to the minority advisory committees, in the fall of 1977, at the request of the Secretary of Commerce, the National Academies of Science established a Committee on the Decennial Census Plans. The first person of color to serve on this committee was one of the first Latino demographers and a UCLA professor, Leobardo F. Estrada, who also served on the Spanish Origin Population Committee. The other person of color on this committee was Eddie N. Williams, president of the Black think tank Joint Center for Political and Economic Studies. He served as the first Black protocol officer at the State Department in 1968 and director of the Center for Policy Study at the University of Chicago (and later vice president for public affairs). To me, this step was similar to the institutionalization of SF State's College of Ethnic Studies. People of color were not confined to minority advisory committees but broadened out to interact with other parts of the census system. In addition, the Population Division of the bureau established a Racial and Ethnic Statistics Program under Nampeo McKenney.

16 "Oral History – Vincent Barabba," *US Census Bureau*, https://www.census. gov/history/pdf/Barabba_Oral_History.pdf, 31-32.

The formal institutional participation of people of color and their organizations and communities in the 1980 Census was energizing. After the conducting of the census, data by racial and Hispanic major classification and for policy-relevant ethnic/nationality subgroups were provided not just to traditional researchers and data junkies but to the communities who provided the data. Data were made accessible to residents to complete their census forms, which created an avenue for civic participation. Census data centers and community based organization partnerships were established. There was even talk of a Hispanic Census Bureau director. In preparation for the 2020 Census, the individual racial and ethnic advisory committees have evolved into National Advisory Committee on Racial, Ethnic and Other Populations, established October 12, 2012.

The experiences of census advisory committees bears lessons consistent with the SF State College of Ethnic Studies. Traditional academic and governmental research views towards communities of color may be summarized as: "I see your community as a subject of my research. What are the problems I see? What are the solutions that I can create based on the assumptions, methods, and findings of my research?" It is an outsider view, not a participant witness one. San Francisco State in the 1960s and the US DHEW and the US Census Bureau in the 1970s, with their respective advisors from communities of color, took a different approach. They looked for common ground. The questions they asked instead included: "How can we together best serve the needs of communities and the mission of our agency/university? What are the organic local needs and wants? How do we learn from one another?" This innovative type of thinking and collaboration is open-minded, multilingual, and on-going. Some disciplines call it "cultural competency." It is not the arrogance of First World, highly-paid "brain on the plane" consultants that land in Third World countries offering high-tech solutions when a low-tech, low-cost solution is required.

As I mention in my 1998 book, *Asian Americans: From Racial Category to Multiple Identities*, organizations such as the Pacific/Asian Coalition and the Federal Advisory Committee on Asian American and Pacific Islander Populations for the 1980 Census are fundamental and instrumental because they represented the very diverse Asian Pacific communities (with the emergence of the Southeast Asian population after the Vietnam War), large population numbers (both US-born and immigrant after the 1965 Immigration Act amendments), and, relatively speaking, large federal monies and staff resources devoted to institutionalizing Asian Pacific Americans as a policy consideration in the federal government. In my view, without this governmental seal of approval and anchor in terms of the federal legislative, legal, and statistical systems on race and ethnicity, many Asian American/people of color initiatives and programs, including Asian American Studies/Ethnic Studies, would be relegated to regional or local status, or perhaps be nonexistent today. This is in part due to the dispersion and heterogeneity of Asian and Pacific American communities, which often lack physical geographic ethnic communities with generations of institutional memory, common experience, and solidarity. This observation is also relevant for other communities of color.

The Smithsonian Institution

Washington, DC is home to the world-famous Smithsonian Institution founded by Englishman James Smithson in 1846 "for the increase and diffusion of knowledge." Until recently, Smithsonian knowledge reflected British and Western European knowledge. With respect to people of color, exhibits were housed in the Museum of Natural History for decades as objects of the world of nature, including the display of skeletal remains of American Indians. In 1989, when an agreement was reached among the Smithsonian, the US Congress, and American Indian representatives to return remains and funerary materials to American Indian tribes for reburial, the institution estimated ownership of 18,600 skeletal remains.[17] Then Secretary Robert Adams stated, "It is wonderful and inevitable. We do so with some regret, but everyone would acknowledge that when you face a collision between human rights and scientific study, then scientific values have to take second place. To do otherwise would suppress the

---

17 Irvin Molotsky, "Smithsonian to Give Up Indian Remains," *New York Times*, September 13, 1989, https://www.nytimes.com/1989/09/13/us/smithsonian-to-give-up-indian-remains.html.

violence against Indians in the westward movement."

Like the Census Bureau did in the 1970s, the Smithsonian Institution began to acknowledge and collaborate with communities of color in the 1980s and 1990s. By January 28, 2010, at its annual program, the Smithsonian Congress of Scholars acknowledged and celebrated the 40th anniversary of the Ethnic Studies movement and its impact on scholarship at the National Museum of the American Indian. Scholars came from various Smithsonian museums, disciplines, and programs, including the Smithsonian Center for Folklife and Cultural Heritage, the National Museum of the American Indian, the National Museum for African American History and Culture (which officially opened its doors in September 2016), the Asian Pacific American Center and the Latino Center. The scholars, led by then Smithsonian Secretary Wayne Clough, Under Secretary Richard Kurin, and senior manager James Early, formally recognized and directly attributed the founding of the discipline of ethnic studies to the 1968–69 SF State strikers and founders of the College of Ethnic Studies. Secretary Clough noted that he was working on his PhD at UC Berkeley during the strike and experienced first-hand the significance of the times.[18]

From West to East back to West and then to Global

Throughout my DC career, I met young people, faculty, and scholar/activists who came up to me at conferences, workshops, and other public events, or when applying for a federal or academic position to say that they were inspired and continue to be motivated by the San Francisco State strike and ethnic studies. In particular, people of color and white women from different areas in the US and abroad would seek folks who looked like them in the federal agencies, universities, and non-profit organizations inside the Washington, DC beltway. Oftentimes, they were the first person in their families to go on to graduate or professional schools and attain mainstream positions. More often than not, they were the only person of color and/or woman in their offices. Just as

---

18 Smithsonian Congress of Scholars, *40 Years of Bringing Cultural Diverse Scholarship to the Smithsonian*, 2:02:48, YouTube Video, posted by "Smithsonian," January 29, 2010, https://www.youtube.com/watch?v=FhPFiAD1A_c.

the current students of ethnic studies from middle school through graduate school eloquently testify to the continuing relevance of ethnic studies to their sense of self and community, the earlier cohorts of college graduates saw their identities and life experiences validated by ethnic studies and/or women's studies. The studies and related programs were their touchstone in alien territory. Sometimes, the touchstone was something as simple as eating ethnic comfort food together or sharing ideas about how to dress for cold weather or driving in the snow with someone who had shared their life journey. Other times, it was to find meaningful answers and calm responses to the questions, "What are you? Where are you from? Are you an affirmative action hire?"

As a career civil servant, I was fortunate to meet folks whose mission was to serve the public. As a federal demographer/statistician I learned much from colleagues who understood statistics as a public good. Moreover, there was a critical mass inside and outside the federal statistical system that advocated for statistical literacy; that is, for the public to understand the data and their appropriate uses. Many of my Black colleagues had been recruited through the Historically Black Colleges (HBC) or the military and been part of the Civil Rights Movement. Certainly at places like DHEW and the Census Bureau, they served as mentors to Third World folks schooled in ethnic studies and arriving from west of the Mississippi. The HBCs had decades earlier provided for young Black men and women the grounding and sense of value, relevance, and service that other people of color experienced through ethnic studies.

At the national level, opportunities opened up to work across disciplines, agencies and sectors (public, private and non-profit), facilitating more inclusion of different life experiences, knowledge, and perspectives. A solid example, in my view, is the work of colleagues across the federal statistical system, both students and professionals via the American Statistical Association (ASA). In 2012, ASA partnered with San Francisco State to host StatFest, an annual one-day conference aimed at encouraging under-represented groups to consider careers and graduate studies in the statistical sciences. StatFest is an ongoing initiative of ASA's Committee on Minorities in Statistics. The College of Ethnic Studies was the SF State lead. Senior leaders from academia, government, and the private sector, many from East of the Mississippi, shared insights and experiences with California students, including a few high schoolers, to help them understand tremendous opportunities in the statistical sciences. Robert Rodriguez, then president of ASA and vice-president of the SAS Institute and notably the first Hispanic president of the ASA since its inception in 1839, gave a special presentation. Sastry Pantula, who served as ASA 2011 president and was the first Asian American president of the association, provided critical contacts. Walter Allen, an ASA member, UCLA professor, dean of graduate studies, and author of *Towards a Brighter Future: College Barriers, Hopes and Plans of Blacks, Latino/a, and Asian American Students in California* (2009), provided keynote remarks. Kenneth Monteiro, then dean of the College of Ethnic Studies, welcomed the attendees from the Bay Area and other California colleges. Students were able to connect directly with possible mentors, faculty and employers. The program noted, "San Francisco State University is proud to host StatFest 2012. SF State's historical longest student-faculty strike in 1968–69 resulted in greater representation of historically discriminated and under-represented populations as students and faculty in higher education. Today SFSU enrolls 30,000 students and consistently ranks in the top 20 nationwide in awarding undergraduate degrees to minorities. With a range of students from almost every state and nearly 100 countries, the University community is a perfect setting for learning to succeed in a pluralistic society and global economy.[19]

In one sense, the recruitment of people of color and white women in the statistical sciences or STEM (Science, Technology, Engineering and Mathematics) is understandable. The STEM disciplines are popularly associated with white boys and men rather than people of color and white women and girls. In a larger sense, however, untold stories are being brought to light that bear witness to other facts. These include, for example, books and films such as *Hidden Figures*, which addresses the critical role of Black women mathematicians at NASA in the success of the space program. White women and people of color have been in

---

19 "StatFest 2012: Promoting Diversity in the Statistical Sciences," October 6, 2012, San Francisco State University.

STEM fields, from NSA cryptographers[20] to scientists at the National institutes for Health to computer programmers for the Army's Electronic Numerical Integrator and computer (ENIAC).[21] Historically, Asian parents in Asia and the Americas encouraged their children to major and work in science, math, technology and engineering on the assumption that they were more "objective" and quantifiable fields where their children would be less likely to be discriminated against compared to the subjective, less quantifiable judgement associated with the social sciences, humanities, and liberal arts. Leaders of the civil rights movement also emphasized higher education careers utilizing the scientific method and inquiry. Former DC Mayor Marion Berry, for example, was a chemistry major.

Before his sudden death in December 2017 at 65 years old, Edwin Lee, the first Asian American mayor of San Francisco and former Asian Law Caucus attorney, advocated not just STEM but STEAM; that is Science, Technology, Engineering, Arts, and Mathematics. Certainly San Francisco and the Bay Area have been a mecca for all sorts of arts, from the San Francisco Sound to the Precita Eyes Muralists, often led by artists of color. Given its natural diverse geography and demography, California has inspired many artists and innovators. In collaborations with other global travelers, young students and their teachers and future employers are rediscovering what old cultures—primarily Third World cultures— recognized before the domination of White Anglo Saxon Protestant culture in the 16th century: the arts and sciences are interconnected. The histories and cultures of various peoples are symbiotic. Demography and geography are equally important. The Golden Children of San Francisco and California encompass Silicon Valley and the San Joaquin Valley. They are inclusive. They have gone out into the nation and world. They went

20 Jennifer Wilcox, *Sharing the Burden: Women in Cryptology during World War II*, (Center for Cryptologic History, National Security Agency, 1998, reprinted 2013), *National Security Agency*, https://www.nsa.gov/about/cryptologic-heritage/historical-figures-publications/publications/wwii/assets/files/sharing_the_burden.pdf.
21 "The History of Women in Computing," *Florida Tech*, https://www.floridatechonline.com/blog/information-technology/the-history-of-women-in-computing/

from West to East and back to West and now are global.

In 2018, the SF State Ethnic Studies experience of a multiracial, multiethnic, multilingual, globally aware populace has come to fruition across the nation. In addition, geographical mobility domestically and internationally has facilitated comparative understanding and analysis. Today, many of the students of the College of Ethnic Studies are not just commuters from San Francisco neighborhoods. Many come from outside the Bay Area, the state, and the country. As SF State commemorates the 50th anniversaries of the 1968 student led strike and the 1969 founding of the School of Ethnic Studies, the discipline of ethnic studies addresses not only internal colonialism but also constant migration, a global diaspora, mixed race populations, and perspectives that vary by cohorts. The Golden Children are not only agents of change but also of continuity.

CHAPTER 5

Golden Children: Agents Of Change and Continuity

At the 40th anniversary commemoration of SF State's BSU/TWLF Strike and founding of the College of Ethnic Studies, Joseph White noted, "the strike changed the legacy of San Francisco State… It changed San Francisco State to a multicultural campus. Those ideas we fought so hard for are now a reality not only at San Francisco State University but all over the United States." [1]

The proportion of people of color in the United States in 2018 is more than a third and comprises the majority in selected areas. There is greater recognition of a very diverse American population by race, culture, language, and nativity. Today, after 50 years, the College of Ethnic Studies at San Francisco State is the only such college not just in the nation but the world. While other universities, especially elite universities, host their rock star ethnic studies professors and a variety of ethnic studies special programs and research centers, no other institution of higher education has a full college with a dean, several departments, majors, minors, budget and building. No other ethnic studies program highlights social justice and serving the everyday needs of everyday people as its core mission. Community service is still integral to students of ethnic studies at San Francisco State, a public university.

As it turns 50 years old, the challenge and opportunity for the College of Ethnic Studies at SF State is not just to remain relevant but to continue leading the way in ensuring access to higher education, nurturing a competitive labor force, graduating responsible citizens, and serving the public good. How does it provide value amidst changes in the role, expectations, and return on investment to higher education? How does it affirm the Golden Children, all our children, at a time when

---

1 Tanya Schevitz, "Remembering the Turbulent Time," *San Francisco Chronicle*, October 26, 2008, https://www.pressreader.com/usa/san-francisco-chronicle/20081026/281951718647536.

American youth are in even greater jeopardy due to a sizable portion of adult leaders no longer seeing themselves as parents protecting their youth or as older brothers and sisters looking out for their younger siblings? In 2018, Mr. Rogers and his neighborhood are barely visible.

As SF State commemorates the 50th anniversaries of the 1968 student-led strike and the 1969 founding of the School of Ethnic Studies, the discipline of ethnic studies addresses not only internal colonialism but also constant migration, a global diaspora, mixed race populations, and perspectives that vary by cohorts. The Golden Children are not only agents of change but also of continuity. When the student-led strike occurred at SF State, the impetus was organic, not abstract nor academic. The movement was driven by students and the needs of the larger community beyond the college. The mission of public schools in a representative democracy was to ensure an informed, civic-minded population and a competent, educated workforce. That mission is questioned and challenged today. Many communities knew that education was the access route for people born without wealth, privilege, and legacy. Especially for a post-industrial, globally-competitive economy, strong human capital was imperative for California. Moreover, the Vietnam War was raging and became the defining moment for that generation of students, in the US and around the world. As stated earlier, the Golden Children were stewards and witnesses. Their stewardship called them to honor the legacy of their ancestors and serve the needs of current and future generations.[2]

As I write this in 2018, American youth and children are again taking center stage, admonishing their elders for not protecting them and future generations. They are running for office and organizing communities at all geographical levels to end violence, from the war in the Middle East to the killing of their classmates in America's schools. They are also raising their voices in the legislative process. In summer 2016, middle and high school students lobbied for Ethnic Studies in California's Department of Education, complementing the SF State TWLF 2016

---

2   Kazmi Torri ed., *The Turning Point- the San Francisco State '68 Strike*, 2014 YouTube Video, 56:01, posted by "laborvideo," December 8, 2014, https://www.youtube.com/watch?v=Qd6-P3kHRBY.

demonstrations in support of ethnic studies at SF State. On April 19, 2018, Bay Area Student Activists lobbied California legislators to enforce stricter gun control laws, such as Assembly Bill 3, which proposed raising the purchase age for long guns, such as rifles and shotguns, from 12 years old to 18 years old. According to their GoFundMe website, "High school students from all over the Bay Area are planning a trip to Sacramento on April 19th. We have resources to bring with us and we want to talk to our Congress about enforcing stricter gun control laws. We are ALL tired of politicians sending their 'thoughts and prayers' and, following the Parkland students, we will be taking our stories and requests straight to the people in charge. We have 10+ private and public schools involved and are excited to sit down and talk. But, we can't get there without YOUR help. We need to pay for our transportation costs (buses) and are asking YOU to help us!"[3] In the spring of 2018, their high school and elementary school teachers are speaking up against dismal state resources to educate America's children and respect the important work of teachers. In West Virginia, a successful state-wide strike that lasted several days inspired teachers in other states to take various actions, from protests to walk outs, in states including Oklahoma, Arizona, Colorado and Kentucky.[4]

Perhaps today's youth can take comfort in the legacy of the 1960s student-led movements, particularly San Francisco State. One major element of this legacy was a serious understanding of what was won, what was lost, and the sacrifices individuals and communities made. There were many individual persons, communities, and organizations involved from all walks of life. A critical mass brought their deep insights and experiences from prior movements, including the labor movement of the 1930s and 1940s, the civil rights movement of the 1950s and 1960s, and the anti-war and farmworkers movements. Several demonstrators and especially the BSU/TWLF leadership had seasoned

3   "Bay Area Student Activists," *GoFundMe*, https://www.gofundme.com/bay-area-student-activists.

4   Cory Turner, Clare Lombardo and Erin Logan, "Teacher Walkouts: a State by State Guide," *NPR Ed: How Learning Happens*, April 25, 2018, https://www.npr.org/sections/ed/2018/04/25/602859780/teacher-walkouts-a-state-by-state-guide.

ties with legitimating institutions of power, notably the US military and the Roman Catholic Church.

In addition, at SF State, for those who had no prior movement or institutional experience, or even awareness and understanding of the dynamics at work, the visceral reality of watching demonstrators and bystanders alike be treated with state-condoned violence day in and day out was the quick learning curve that motivated them to take a stand on the strike. This involvement occurred through individual unsung heroes and heroines, through membership with BSU/TWLF student organizations at SF State and other campuses, and through representatives of various local communities and community organizations, especially youth-led ones, including the Black Panthers, the Brown Berets, and American Indians of All Tribes. Along with individual consciences, there were collective memory, shared experiences, and a collective conscience. Today's youthful agents of change and continuity are beginning to demonstrate the same vibrant and unified presence of the 1968–69 golden children—powerful images of both whites and people of color standing together. This is legacy that Golden Children today can take to heart.

As BSU and TWLF Central Committee leader Nesbitt Crutchfield presciently stated in 1969, "The strike is over, but the struggle continues." That is, due vigilance is ongoing and victory is never final. While finite, the strike's impact was not fleeting. It is embodied in the College of Ethnic Studies and every student, staff, faculty or community member associated with the college in negotiations over the strike demands—the principles for self-determination and relevant education as manifested in a "School of Third World Studies." These principles must be articulated and lived in the continuing maintenance and maturity of ethnic studies.

Similarly, in a 2018 interview with KQED, Abby Ginzberg, co-producer and director of *Agents of Change*, was asked what she thought was the biggest lesson to be learned from the campus protests 50 years later. "The main lesson, I believe, is to not take any of these successes for granted and to understand that each generation may have to fight for these gains all over again. Black and ethnic studies programs are now taken for granted by many students on campuses around the country.

Learning that they were forged in struggle by students, not only at S.F. State and Cornell but at over 1,000 campuses in the late 1960s and early 1970s, is critical to efforts to preserve them. Another part of the S.F. State legacy is that in spite of the intervening 50 years, racism is still present on college campuses. Inclusion is still a distant goal, and many campuses are experiencing some of the same issues that led to the protests at S.F. State and Cornell. So in a word, we still have a long way to go."[5]

A second element of this legacy was that the creation of Ethnic Studies at SF State was not just unique but innovative. The SF State strike and founding of ethnic studies were not isolated events or outliers. Together they were one large data point—a significant milestone—among the acts of resistance on college campuses locally and globally against the war in Southeast Asia and the institutional subordination and segregation of peoples of color. This point in time stands out and is remembered uniquely because a numerical minority of working class and middle income students of color were leading the resistance, supported by a majority of white students and faculty, their families, communities, and off campus networks. Not only were they protesting the war, they were also warning of the deteriorating gap between the educational and employment opportunities for people of color compared to whites and the inequitable adherence to rule of law and due process that subjugated people of color. The innovative process of change that occurred after the strike was an ethnic studies program created by the students and their communities, not by traditional experts within an educational system that was serving them poorly, or not at all.

A third significant part of SF State's legacy is that there was no lag time between the settlement of the strike and the planning for and implementation of the then School of Ethnic Studies. The strike agreement was sealed in March 1969. Classes were offered immediately in the various departments of ethnic studies in fall 1969. This is no small accomplishment.

---

5   Adam Grossberg and JoeBill Munoz, "New Documentary Looks Back at S.F. State Strike on 50th Anniversary," *KQED News*, https://www.kqed.org/news/11649871/new-documentary-looks-back-at-sf-state-strike-on-50th-anniversary.

The Golden Children of today are the TWLF 2016 students and their cohort, their younger siblings made up of immigrants and refugees, with or without legal documents, whose home and allegiance is to the United States, and the children across this nation who stand up to violence in all its manifestations, daring to challenge their elders to be responsible leaders. They are agents of both change and continuity.

Continuity

Before assessing the changes that today's Golden Children face and respond to, it is useful to summarize the several strands of continuity they share with yesterday's Golden Children. The most striking examples are the news photos of 1968–69 TWLF strikers standing in solidarity with the 2016 TWLF Strikers and the media coverage of children in elementary and secondary schools from the San Francisco Unified School District traveling to the California State Department of Education in Sacramento to demand ethnic studies in their classrooms. In post-film discussions for *Agents of Change*, Abby Ginzberg and I have noted that many current students speak about the specific challenges they face in terms of racism on their campuses and the efforts to preserve and expand, rather than cut back, their Ethnic Studies departments and programs. As students of ethnic studies, children and youth today are learning about and understanding the reasons for the SF State strike and the wide reach of the College of Ethnic studies beyond campus.

Second is the continuity across generations of students, faculty, and community who believe and defend the idea that the purpose of public education, from pre-school to graduate school, is to produce educated citizens and a competitive workforce; for example, by testifying before city boards of education and state departments of education for adequate resources and relevant education.[6] Public state universities all over the US, including SF State and the CSU system, are critical, as they are in the middle position between community colleges and the elite flagship university research centers such as UCs. The majority of college students will be educated by the community colleges and state universities. In

---

6 *Agents of Change*, DVD, directed by Abby Ginzberg and Frank Dawson, (2016; Los Angeles, CA: Films with a Purpose, 2016).

the 20th century, they provided the human capital for a solid and sizable middle class, a major historical achievement that is barely recognized or appreciated today.

Third is the continuing legacy of parents and communities sacrificing for their children's education. This is particularly true for working class families whose children are the first to attend college. In turn, children understand and respect those sacrifices of their elders. There is a collective memory, shared experiences, and a collective conscience across generations. Finally, despite negative media 24/7, the demand for self-determination and relevant education persists across the nation. What continues today is strong belief that children and youth, with the support of the adults in their lives, can be effective agents of change

A poignant example, in my view, are the recent comments of Lester Holt, NBC Nightly News anchor who covered the 50th anniversary of Rev. Dr. Martin Luther King, Jr.'s assassination in April 1968. He was asked whether reporting on this historical anniversary changed his perspective on the milestone nature of his appointment as the first Black network news anchor. He answered, "We all have to be reminded of where we came from and how we got here and the doors that were opened up through a lot of sacrifices. It's reminded me of the shoulders that I stand on, that I had the opportunity to do whatever I wanted in life. I think what's really made me focus on the impact of this role at this time is the number of people who have reached out about their children, children of color, who watch me, that's the stuff that comes full circle." [7]

Full circle can also apply to the challenge of higher education to provide access for more students in 2018 and beyond. California's population is projected to soon be 40 million, which means, as in 1968, the challenge of providing higher education to more students continues. The need for higher education is greater than in 1968, not only for American youth but also adults who must adapt to a world of continuous learning and ever-evolving means of communication, including mastery of low and high tech social media.

---

[7] Daniel D'Addario, "6 Questions," *TIME*, April 23, 2018, 56.

Change

A very visible change for today's students at SF State (and other campuses) is that the university is no longer a commuter college. As of fall 2016, while over half (59%) resided in the Bay Area at the time of their college application, a sizable segment (22%) were recruited from southern California. Five percent were from Central California and seven percent from Northern California. One percent were from other states, while international students comprised 6%. Not surprisingly, given the strike agreement, SF State continues to be a leader for a diverse student body with the unique distinction that over half are Asian or Hispanic. In terms of faculty, while white faculty are still a majority of tenure/tenure track positions, Asian Americans hold a sizable number of such positions. Many students today, unlike the 1968–69 alumni, do not go home to the San Francisco neighborhoods where they grew up. The organic, grassroots origins and motivation have lessened over time.

While homelessness is a decades-long reality in San Francisco, the reality of homeless students has become more visible today due to escalating real estate prices and the spiraling costs of education, which are structural issues beyond the control of individual students or SF State. Another change is that students in the CSU and UC systems are faced with food insecurity. Again, this is a structural issue. Whereas in the 1960s, there was no tuition (student fees were around $50 a semester) and many students on work study could rent an apartment and buy groceries, that is not true in 2018 or the foreseeable future. Another systemic change is the corporatization of education, especially public higher education.

The role of higher education is undergoing change in the 21st century. In the 20th century and in particular 1968, it was clear that a public state university's purpose was to educate its youth to be productive residents and citizens. Educating its children was an investment in human capital and the future. The goal was to be middle class. For California, there were big dividends given its diverse economy that included such industries as agriculture, Silicon Valley, film and television, military-industrial research, the space program, and healthcare. California was considered one of the top ten economies in the world. In education, the gold standard for assessments was the California Achievement Test and the public, free University of California system was ranked number one. That changed in 1978 with Proposition 13. While today California is ranked the sixth largest economy in the world, the rankings of California students and public higher education have fallen. Instead there exists a growing gap among a very small proportion of the ultra rich and everyone else along with a disappearing middle class. For ethnic studies in the 20th century, opening the channels of upward mobility through educational opportunity was in reach. In the 21st century, this possibility is problematic for ethnic studies and other areas of study.

Higher education today is an industry from pre-school to post-graduate education that continues to spew products of credentialization for high fees without a clear return on investment. It perpetuates consumers-in-debt rather than producers-of-credit. In 1968–69, higher education, especially public higher education, was a proven path to middle class status in the US. In 2018, students and their parents incur student debts for undergraduate, graduate and professional degrees with no guarantees of permanent jobs that offer a living wage and benefits. The challenge for ethnic studies is staying true to its core as costs of higher education continue. For students and faculty, the cost of undergraduate and graduate education are steep; five-digit student loans are not unusual. For faculty, tenure-track positions are at a premium. Post docs, teaching assistants, lecturer positions, and adjunct professorships do not pay a living wage or provide benefits, let alone lead to a permanent position with an office and institutional affiliation. The ability to manage both academic responsibilities and community service in an era of careerism and specialization (which becomes obsolete with the next innovation or hot issue) is challenging. The expectations and rewards of higher education continue to be traditional and evolving. For example, publishing in first-tier professional publications is still a priority but must be accompanied by presence in social and popular media; winning grants and contracts is complemented by other development and fundraising efforts. Faculty are expected to travel nationally and internationally to conferences and to conduct research elsewhere. The equivalent for lecturers and adjunct professors means traveling across various campuses for part-time appointments. Such conditions reward mobility and volatility over stability and grounding.

While SF State COES has control of its staff and faculty, other ethnic studies programs sometimes are housed in more traditional disciplines that define who gets hired and who is considered an expert in ethnic studies. The expanding role of other institutions, particularly museums, in defining educational content, including ethnic studies, further waters down the goal of educating for the people. Instead, content is produced for the elite audiences with narrow areas of expertise perpetuated by white, Western tradition. The meritocracy and technocratic elite, rather than public service and the public interest, hold sway in these legitimating institutions of power. With this environment, it is possible that there can be a re-segregation back to a traditional discipline. Not unlike the Chicago school, the re-segregation envisions white experts in ethnic studies. Programs are called "ethnic studies," for example, in small private colleges in the Northeast and public universities in the Midwest but do not bear much resemblance to the ethnic studies programs that exist where there is a sizable portion of people of color. Their focus is intellectual reproduction rather than community service or civic engagement. Not unlike the publishing industry, the education industry promotes people of color (not necessarily American) and others who have made their marks as token superstars in elite or private universities. These scholars get more publicity and funding as comparative ethnic studies scholars and researchers than those in public universities. Oftentimes, these colleagues do not readily—or almost reluctantly—acknowledge the role of SF State, the state universities, and the community colleges in the birth of ethnic studies, especially omitting the central role of community service to an ethnic studies education. It appears that such programs are more intent on producing academic careerists whose loyalty is to the institution. This pattern is more like museum experts, whose knowledge is abstract and levels away from the lives of ordinary people. Becoming academic like a museum can easily remove students and faculty from real people and the human condition, moving from a subject in the real world to an object in a manufactured one. The move is towards greater anonymous digital learning with reduction in person-to-person interaction in physical space.

This is an unintended, but perhaps anticipated consequence, of bringing forth systemic educational change that required personal and collective sacrifices. It is difficult to swallow this reality for those unsung heroines and heroes who sacrificed by going on strike, facing imprisonment, and losing income and employment.

I believe that the continuing and changing legacy of SF State's Golden Children from BSU/TWLF 1968–89, TWLF 2016 and beyond, can be understood via Material Remembrances, Academic Institutional Contributions and Innovations, and Continuity and Change across Human Relationships.

Material Remembrances

The legacy of the BSU/TWLF 1968–69 Golden Children is remembered by occasional commemorations such as the 40th and 50th anniversaries of the founding of Ethnic Studies. Any material remembrance on campus is modest, in line with SF State being a public state university that serves the children of parents who are local residents and tax payers. One of the material remembrances is a plaque atop a rock in the middle of campus under a grove of gorgeous, huge, decades-old California Cypress. The plaque is not readily seen as students and faculty walk across campus. If one is on the edge of the Commons facing towards the old BSS building on 19th Avenue with the J. Paul Leonard Library on the right and the Cesar Chavez Student Center in the back, one can see two plaques atop rocks. The plaque on the left, placed atop a larger rock, is dedicated to various American civil rights leaders from 1954 to 1968. The plaque on the right, framed by pink camellia bushes, simply says: "November 6, 1968......... November 4, 2008 / Connect the Dots."

These remembrances in the center of campus were part of the 40th anniversaries commemorations (strike and founding of ethnic studies) with the stalwart collaboration of then SF State President Robert Corrigan.

Another remembrance is the Ethnic Studies/Psychology building. It was the Psychology Building in 1968. When faculty, staff and students established ethnic studies in 1969, the first floor of the Psychology Building housed the departmental offices for Asian American Studies,

Black Studies, La Raza Studies, Native American Studies, and the office of the Dean of Ethnic Studies. The renaming of the building occurred while Tomas Almaguer was dean of the College of Ethnic Studies and Ken Monteiro was dean of Human Resources. They worked with students from Ethnic Studies and Psychology to make this change.[8]

Third is the Cesar Chavez Student Center. In 1968–69, there was no student center. Student organizations were housed in small wooden buildings that several TWLF leaders nicknamed "the huts." This name was an acknowledgement of the ongoing Vietnam War. It also evoked the line, "Our office is a hut in the forest" by writer William Pomeroy in *The Forest: A Personal Record of the Huk Guerilla Struggle in the Philippines* (1965). The huts stood between the library and cafeteria. As mentioned in Chapter 2, the other student site for gathering was Ecumenical House, which was across 19th Avenue. In 1975, the Chavez Center opened in the heart of the campus and currently houses more than 20 student organization offices, food and beverage vendors, the SFSU Bookstore, and various meeting rooms and event spaces. The latter include the Richard Oakes Multicultural Center, the Rosa Parks Rooms, Jack Adams Hall, and Malcolm X Plaza. There are several murals at the student center on the contributions of Cesar Chavez, Malcolm X, Edward Said, and The Filipino Community, among others. These serve as icons to connect present and future students to the student-led strike and a rich history of social movements that included people of color as leaders and unsung heroes and heroines.[9]

Fourth are the collection of videotapes by local and national media, notably KQED, KPIX/CBS, KRON/NBC that record day-by-day the events from the beginning to the end of the strike. As mentioned in Chapter 2, the KQED 16 millimeter tapes were stored for years by Belva Davis and KRON/NBC political editor Rollin Post until they could be properly archived at SF State J. Paul Leonard Library. This painstaking work was done by a team led by Helene Whitson in The KQED Film

---

8 Kenneth Monteiro, personal communication with author, March 16, 2018.
9 "Murals at SF State—Counter Hegemonic Narratives of Politics and Survival," *SFSU COES*, https://diva.sfsu.edu/collections/coes/bundles/189536.

Archive Preservation Project and described in Christian Alvarado's documentary.[10] The added value of these archived videotapes is that ethnic studies students and others, such as organized labor media, used these archives extensively in conducting research for projects inside and outside the classroom. *Agents of Change* directors and co-producers Abby Ginzberg and Frank Dawson acknowledge that having such treasure was instrumental for producing the documentary. Lesser-known but thoughtful videos were done by SFSF/COES students. These include *Activist State - Documentary SF State Strike* by Jonathan Craig;[11] *The Turning Point - the San Francisco State '68 Strike;*[12] *SFSU TWLF 2016 Hunger Strikers Demands at May 9, 2016 Rally;*[13] and *Danny Glover Speaks Out in Support of SF Ethnic Studies Hunger Strikers.*[14]

During the strike, perhaps the greatest material remembrance and symbol of free speech and academic freedom was the Speakers Platform. It is depicted in many of the television newsreels of the period. It was in front of where the Cesar Chavez Student Center resides today, bordering the large grassy area of "The Commons." For part of the 50th anniversary commemoration of the strike and the founding of ethnic studies, SF State librarian Meredith Eliassen and 2017–2018 Associated Students President Jackie Foley have taken the lead to create a digital timeline of SF State that will feature strike images, including the emergence of the Speakers Platform. For example, this project includes an image titled

---

10 Cristian Alvarado, "On Strike! The Birth of the College of Ethnic Studies."

11 Jonathan Craig, *Activist State: A Documentary About The 1968 San Francisco Student Strike*, 2009 YouTube Video, 26:16, posted by "Jonathan Craig," February 10, 2013, https://www.youtube.com/watch?v=aoPmb-9ctGc.

12 Kazmi Torri ed., *The Turning Point- the San Francisco State '68 Strike*, 2014 YouTube Video, 56:01, posted by "laborvideo," December 8, 2014, https://www.youtube.com/watch?v=Qd6-P3kHRBY.

13 Labor Video Project, *SFSU TWLF 2016 Hunger Striker's Demands At May 9, 2016 Rally*, 2016 YouTube Video, 7:54, posted by "laborvideo," May 10, 2016, https://www.youtube.com/watch?v=umgRO_Hwqgg.

14 *Danny Glover Speaks Out In Support Of SF State Ethnic Studies Hunger Strikers*, 2016 YouTube Video, 7:25, posted by "laborvideo," May 9, 2016, https://www.youtube.com/watch?v=G965nQn_g1E

"Students gathered at Speakers Platform."[15] The Speakers Platform was a student design coming out of the Speakers Bureau established around 1950.[16]

Off campus, I would argue that one of the most endearing material remembrances is Alcatraz Island. While the 1969 occupation of Alcatraz by Indians of All Tribes ended in 1971, Alcatraz affirms the past, present and future of the Golden Children in California and the US as a whole. The National Park Service has a long and seasoned track record in cultural interpretation of the American experience in all of its diversity over time and space. Based on the book *We Hold the Rock: The Indian Occupation of Alcatraz* by Troy Johnson, the National Park Service produced the award-winning film, *We Hold the Rock*, which includes perspectives from Indians, their allies, and the federal government.[17]

As mentioned, earlier, some of the organizers of the occupation of Alcatraz were SF State students in the ethnic studies program, namely Richard Oakes, Wilma Mankiller, and other American Indian Studies students. They worked with other Indian university student groups and American Indian organizations and allies, initially in California, then across the nation. In 2018, along with the water tanks and other buildings re-painted to signify Indian presence, the orientation film to Alcatraz includes the history of the local Ohlones, who preceded the Spaniards and Americans, and the general history of American Indians at the time of the Alcatraz occupation. At the entrance to one of the first information buildings, visitors are greeted by a wall with a white cloth bounded by four poles that has a painting of a teepee and the words, "We Are Still Here." While there is no American Indian Cultural Center on the island, which was one of the demands of the occupation, there is an exhibit, "We Hold the Rock," featuring various American Indians, many of whom were and continue to be student, faculty, and community leaders. In collaboration with the National Park Service, this

---

15 "Students gathered at the Speakers Platform," *SFSU COES*, https://diva.sfsu.edu/collections/timelineproject/bundles/232461.

16 Meredith Eliassen, personal communication with author, March 16, 2018.

17 *We Hold the Rock*, 2014 YouTube Video, 25:39, posted by "Golden Gate National Recreation Area," October 7, 2014, https://www.youtube.com/watch?v=gEmae2PsWJI.

exhibit was created by the American Indian Studies Department, The Cesar E. Chavez Institute, and Richard Oakes Multicultural Center of San Francisco State.

Academic Institutional Contributions

The academic institutional contributions of SF State's COES are not always recognized if one views higher education through a traditional lens. These institutional contributions include establishing ethnic studies as a discipline, developing ethnic studies as a profession with new career paths, the importance of direct community service carried out by a public state university, and the relevance of a public state university in producing engaged citizens and a competitive labor force. Additionally, a strategic contribution was that immediately after the strike settlement on March 20, 1969, students, staff, faculty, and community representatives began formal meetings with the administration to develop courses and hire faculty so the studies could start as fully staffed and funded departments in fall 1969.

As noted by the Smithsonian Congress of Scholars in 2010 in Chapter Four, SF State COES established Ethnic Studies as an academic discipline and legitimate area of scholarship, which brought the recognition of people of color in the university from the perspectives of these peoples, not from outside observers or experts. SF State COES had the particular advantage of already having a few people of color in traditional disciplines who understood and shared similar life experiences with the strikers and founders of ethnic studies, such as Bea Medicine in Anthropology. In addition, COES utilized respected community leaders who were experts in their field, such as architect Philip Choy, to come share their knowledge and insight. This is similar to experts in industry, who do not necessarily have graduate degrees but serve as adjunct faculty. Such scholarship, grounded in the real world outside of campus, affirmed interdisciplinary perspectives with tangible results and areas of scholarship not necessarily defined or acknowledged by academics.

The ethnic studies field is unique as an educational experience that redefines the lives of people of color from their own perspectives. This is implemented through the cooperative efforts of students, faculty, and members of the community who are invested in meaningful education that provides resources and curricula to the university and the community-at-large. Decades of educational and psychological research, as well as real-life educational experiences, affirm that students from pre-school to post-graduate school need to connect with people who look like them and have similar life experience. A powerful example through the decades is high school math teacher, Jaime Escalante, who motivated his working class, mainly Hispanic, students at James A. Garfield High School in East Los Angeles to excel and reach their potential and pass AP Calculus exams. This true story was made into the 1988 award-winning film, *Stand and Deliver*, as well as a book by education reporter Jay Matthews titled *Escalante: the Best Teacher in America*. COES curriculum fosters both a comprehensive understanding of the unique experiences of American Indians, Asian Americans, Blacks, and Latina/Latinos in the United States, and intersectional analysis amongst the different communities.[18] There is recognition and a respect for the diverse intellectual traditions and cultural expressions of scholars, activists, and artists of color and indigenous people throughout the United States that predate a 16th century White Anglo Saxon Protestant world view.

SF State COES is also a leader in ensuring Ethnic Studies as a profession. One of the successes of SF State is that a critical mass of student, faculty, and staff strikers transitioned from being strikers to serving as planning committee members to set up ethnic studies. In fact, a few are still in the college as staff or faculty in 2018. Immediately after the strike settlement on March 20, 1969, students, staff, faculty, and community representatives began formal meetings with the administration to develop courses and hire faculty so the studies could start with base staffing and funding for all departments in fall 1969. Creating a college from scratch meant the importance of original research, often applied research, entailing new innovative research methods for identifying and cataloguing primary sources, conducting oral interviews, training participant witnesses, and creating memoirs of people of color juxtaposed with formal traditional research assumptions and methods of

---

18   "About," *SFSU*, https://ethnicstudies.sfsu.edu/content/about-college-ethnic-studies.

outsider experts.

While hundreds of people have directly benefited from SF State College of Ethnic Studies as students, faculty, staff, and friends over fifty years, COES also inspired and enhanced the careers and callings of thousands of people in the United States and abroad. Many people of color domestic and foreign, as well as white folks, have benefitted from the expansion of higher education curriculum and employment positions created by the new and innovative discipline of ethnic studies. The various conferences, workshops, publications, art work, and documentaries on acknowledging, understanding, and teaching diverse students, preparing relevant curricula, creating degree programs, and identifying and hiring culturally competent ethnic studies faculty, as well as a host of diversity consultants, artists and entrepreneurs exist and expand because of the foundation and affirmation provided by SF State COES. SF State COES remains the institutional embodiment, day in and day out, of the reality that young people organize and unite organically from their grassroots neighborhoods with the support of their parents, communities, businesses, and religious leaders.

A documentary such as *Agents of Change*, featuring Cornell University in 1969, is incomplete and insufficient without understanding the larger powerful context of San Francisco State 1968. As co-producer Abby Ginzberg noted, "When you look at the outcome, it was the creation of black studies and Latino studies and, later, LGBT studies across the country. The difference with the young leaders today, like those in the 'I, Too, Am Harvard' movement, is that they have fabulous people of color as professors who wouldn't have had a job back then. We have whole new academic disciplines that have come out of people wanting to study issues of black and related themes, and that was one of the central demands of the protests." Co-producer Frank Dawson added, "A number of places have gone away from recruiting from urban centers, and returned to the suburbs. The Black students are once again from the middle class. There are students of color, but if you look at the socioeconomic background, it's a really different focus. There are many fewer hardcore urban students."[19]

While the importance of direct community service by the university was pioneered by the SF State Experimental College, it became institutionalized with the establishment of the School of Ethnic Studies. Direct service to community was and is still very key to the identity of the COES. Such service is not carried out as a missionary or outside observer/ expert but as a community member. This is an innovation of life outside the bubble of the traditional ivory tower. It has relevance to everyday people, as opposed to a Hayakawa view of the university as a place for pursuing singular faculty interest and the life of the mind.[20] This affirms that charity begins at home as an organic part of daily experience. The staying power of community-based organizations means that COES has networks and infrastructure outside academia. Each of the departments of the COES can attest to various community-university initiatives. These examples are available on their respective websites and the programs of the COES annual Celebration Awards Program from 2009, 2010, 2011, 2012, 2013, 2014, and 2015. One example of note as it, too, celebrates longevity of service, is the community newspaper, *El Tecolote*. *El Tecolote* began as a spring 1970 project in a La Raza Studies class at San Francisco State University created by Juan Gonzales. The first issue was published during the summer on August 24, 1970. Professor Gonzales, who also served as chair of La Raza Studies, developed the class as a way to channel more Latinos into journalism. At that time Latinos and other people of color were virtually invisible in the major newsrooms. The newspaper soon moved into the Mission District, becoming a training ground for advocacy journalism and playing an important role in the community by covering issues often ignored by the mainstream press. From the beginning, *El Tecolote* has been a community effort, powered by donations and an army of dedicated volunteers. Today it is an award-winning biweekly publication with an owner-occupied office building,

---

19 Nathaniel Horwitz, "An Interview with 'Agents of Change' Producers," *Martha Vineyard Times*, August 12, 2015, http://www.mvtimes. com/2015/08/12/an-interview-with-agents-of-change-producers/.
20 Labor Video Project, "'The Turning Point' The San Francisco State '68 Strike," 2015 YouTube Video, 56:01, posted by "laborvideo," December 8, 2014, https://www.youtube.com/watch?v=Qd6-P3kHRBY.

a circulation of 10,000, and a small paid staff. It is the longest-running Spanish/English bilingual newspaper in California. It continues to welcome COES students to work as part of their community service or fieldwork/academic research. *El Tecolote* is also a member of the San Francisco Neighborhood Newspaper Association and a founding member of New America Media, a national network of ethnic news media.[21]

The "Introduction to Japanese American Community" course provided student volunteers for existing organizations in Japantown and helped create new ones to serve a range of community members. These ranged from the Japanese Community Youth Council (JCYC) to Kimochi, which was founded in 1971 as one of the first senior service centers, continuing the Japanese tradition of care and support for seniors. This was three years before the formal creation of the federal National Institute of Aging on October 7, 1974. According to Rich Wada a striker and member of the Japanese American Studies Planning Group, "In my personal view Asian America (sic) Studies and Ethnic Studies had a significant impact on the various ethnic communities. For San Francisco's Japantown and the Japanese American community, many concerned people were responsible for the creation of new community services and advocacy organizations. In San Francisco the organizations that can trace their founding directly to AAS community involvement are Kimochi, Japanese Community Youth Council (JCYC), The Center for Japanese American Studies-now the Japanese American National Library." [22]

SF State COES also affirms the continuing relevance and responsibility of a public state university to produce engaged citizens and a competitive labor force. A major strike demand and continuing initiative of COES is to admit students from working class neighborhoods, primarily youth of color, and non-traditional students, many being the first in their families to go to college. Instead of being marginal, they are groomed to be involved in the mainstream, to become leaders on campus, in their communities, and in the larger society. To ensure that

---

21 Juan Gonzales, personal correspondence with author, May 3, 2018.
22 Richard Wada, personal communication with author, May 12, 2018.

COES students continue and complete their studies, various types of academic support and financial assistance have been generated. One is the *James A. Hirabayashi Person for All Seasons Scholarship*. Named in memory of the first dean of the College of Ethnic Studies and also a former Dean of Undergraduate Studies, this scholarship annually supports one undergraduate and one graduate student who are considering careers that are interdisciplinary and in public service. The *D. Phillip McGee Memorial Scholarship*, named for the third dean, is awarded to upperclassmen, with preference given to economically disadvantaged students committed to helping others with similar backgrounds. The *Betty Parent Achievement Award* honors the first Alaska Native woman to earn a PhD and the first Alaska Native woman to obtain tenure as a full professor who taught in the American Indian Studies Department. This award, covering books and supplies, is for outstanding graduate and undergraduate students committed to working with an American Indian tribal community, nation and/or organization. The newest form of supporting students of ethnic studies is the Kenneth P. Monteiro–Associated Students Scholarship Endowment in Ethnic Studies in honor of Dr. Kenneth P. Monteiro, who mentored many student leaders at SF State. In February 2018, the Associated Students bestowed on Dr. Monteiro an honorary membership to their board of directors for his outstanding service and dedication to student advocacy and empowerment. The Kenneth P. Monteiro–Associated Students Scholarship Endowment in Ethnic Studies shall recognize and provide financial assistance to students who, like Dr. Monteiro, are committed to advancing and empowering our diverse communities.

The COES has also been a leader in the California Task Force on the Advancement of Ethnic Studies within the California State University (CSU) system and the CSU Ethnic Studies Council. As of April 2018, 22 of the 23 CSUs offer ethnic studies courses. According to Dylan Rodriguez, the chair of the ethnic studies department at the University of California, Riverside, "the departments that sprang up all over the country are the product of ordinary social and student movement organizing. That sets them apart from all other institutions in higher education."[23]

Given the strategic role of CSUs between the community college local system and the UC state-wide system and the fact that CSUs impact the greatest number of students in higher education and the workforce, such expansion of ethnic studies is promising. In a July 13, 2016 press release, the task force noted, "Contrary to a common impression held prior to this study, the data in this study demonstrate that student interest and enrollment are not waning in ethnic studies but rather increasing. Specifically, the data in this study demonstrate that the student-faculty ratio in ethnic studies courses is rising, indicating a higher student enrollment per class offered. However, although interest is rising, enrollment may drop wherever the number of faculty is insufficient to accommodate increased interest. Therefore, it is important for the CSU and its campuses to address expanding student interest as part of advancing ethnic studies as a necessary component in the student's education as vital to the university's realization of its mission. The Task Force: Provides an overview of the origins and histories of ethnic studies programs in the CSU within a national context. Identifies the trends in the campus' programs within the context of institutional support and the national climate, particularly over the past 8-10 years Propose system-wide recommendations that are responsive to the mission of the CSU and to the needs of our students, California, and society in general. This includes examining our degrees, majors, and minors/concentrations as well as the resources."[24] As of 2018, the task force is focusing on four areas of action: increasing access to ethnic studies courses, utilizing ethnic studies programs as a gateway to deepening the educational experience, strengthening connections between ethnic studies programs and the wider community, and integrating the ethnic studies programs in the larger picture of campus climate and culture.

Several years ago, San Francisco Unified School District (SFUSD)

---

23 Kristina Rizga, "Black Studies Matter," *Mother Jones*, May 19, 2016, http://www.motherjones.com/politics/2016/05/ethnic-studies-agents-of-change-documentary-san-francisco.

24 Timothy P. White, "Report of the California State University Task Force on the Advancement of Ethnic Studies," *CalState*, July 13, 2016, https://www.calstate.edu/AcadAff/ethnicstudiesreport.pdf.

voted to create ethnic studies classes for high school students to provide them with a culturally and community responsive classroom experience. The district partnered with the College of Ethnic Studies (COES) at San Francisco State University (SFSU). Preliminary research proves that the collaboration is working. It is a collaboration that serves as a milestone for the historical student strike at San Francisco State, showing the growth of Ethnic Studies departments, programs and courses throughout the nation.

According to a research study done by the Stanford Graduate School of Education, this higher education and secondary education partnership is proving to be remarkably successful.[25] Specifically, the study compared academic outcomes for students who took ethnic studies classes and those who did not. The former exhibited improved student attendance and increased academic performance. According to Allyson Tintiangco-Cubales, Professor of Asian American Studies at the COES, who served as the Academic Advisor and worked with SFUSD teachers to create the curriculum, "The goal was designed not just to develop curriculum but to develop the teachers teaching the curriculum as well. The students learn things that are relevant to their lives and they are engaged in the material. But they are also learning to use that material to develop their academic skills whether in reading, writing, critical research or critical analysis. Ethnic Studies also goes beyond the classroom and provides an education that students can use to improve their lives and the lives of the people in the community."[26]

Classes focus on teaching American history through the lenses of race, ethnicity, nationality, and cultural identity. They are designed to allow students to comprehend the academic material in the context of their shared experiences, preparing them to succeed while embracing their ethnic identities and solving problems in their communities and society at large. Aimee Riechel, a teacher at Mission High School has been

---

25 Brooke Donald, "Stanford Study Suggest Academic Benefits to Ethnic Studies Courses," *Stanford Report*, January 12, 2016, http://news.stanford.edu/news/2016/january/ethnic-studies-benefits-011216.html.

26 "College of Ethnic Studies and SFUSD Collaborate: Students Succeed," *SFSU*, https://ethnicstudies.sfsu.edu/content/stanford-university-study-affirms-ethnic-studies

developing curriculum and teaching 9th grade ethnic studies for nearly seven years. The school offers five ethnic study classes at the 9th grade level and a 12th grade ethnic studies honors class. "Many students who have struggled in English class have enjoyed writing in the ethnic studies courses. Reading skills have improved. They actually enjoy struggling with the work assignments." Riechel remembers the impact the class had on one particular student. "He was failing in many of his other classes but consistently earned A's in ethnic studies class. I was surprised that he wasn't as successful in other classes."[27] These students now succeed in ethnic studies and in their other classes. The Stanford study found that the attendance for those enrolled in ethnic studies classes increased by 21 percentage points, GPA by 1.4 grade points and credits earned by 23. It also found significant effects on GPA specific to math and science achievement, suggesting that exposure to ethnic studies could increase performance in science, technology, engineering and mathematics (STEM). The data were gathered from three high school classes in the SFUSD participating in ethnic studies from 2010 to 2014.

Institutional innovations

What makes SF State COES institutionally innovative is understanding that it was here to endure, evolve, and adapt as needed without losing sight of the core mission and sacrifices that birthed it. These innovations include: 1) being a college instead of individual departments or research centers since its inception and continuing to be so in its sixth decade; 2) presenting ethnic studies classes, from the start, as courses to fulfill general education requirements, 3) requiring direct community service, 4) providing course work that prepares students for relevant leadership in the wider society; 5) being open and inclusive over the years by, for example, expanding into emerging areas of scholarship such as Pacific Islander Studies, Arab, Palestinian and Muslim studies, and Diaspora Studies; 5) facilitating ethnic studies as one of two majors in a double major/double degree program, encouraging an interdisciplinary perspective; and 6) modeling leadership as a group role rather than an individual role, as evidenced by widely utilizing the consensus model.

---

27 Ibid.

The premise of the student-led strike was "United we stand. Divided we fall." Leaders of the TWLF Central Committee and the Ethnic Studies Planning Committees modeled this core belief. They understood the debilitating consequences of competitive strategies that divide and conquer or that set up individual leaders/celebrity scholars. They were stronger as one program rather than as separate departments or programs or research centers. Leaders of TWLF 2016 and current staff and faculty continue this unified front and resistance. What SF State uniquely did was to institutionalize disparate efforts across various racial/ethnic groups and define them as a Third World College, (later negotiated into a School of Ethnic Studies), with various departments and Full Time Equivalent (FTE) resources. It offered an institutional alternative to Eurocentric higher education. Ending the four-month strike and establishing ethnic studies at SF State was accomplished by collaboration and negotiation among students, faculty administration, staff, community organizations, organized labor, businesses, government representatives and institutions of faith.

Starting first with Asian American Studies courses, ethnic studies courses were institutionalized immediately by fulfilling general education requirements. The general education courses in 1968–69 were part of the undergraduate liberal arts focus for lower classmen, which allowed them to draw from a range of courses in order to be well-rounded citizens ready to solve real-world problems that were dynamic and interdisciplinary. This was attractive not just for freshmen and sophomores but other students interested in ethnic studies or sympathetic to the struggle to attain ethnic studies. Almost from the beginning, enrollment was solid. According to long time Asian American Studies curriculum planner and lecturer Malcolm Collier, this requirement allows students, especially students from the different ethnic communities, to explore their own histories, communities, and cultures in the United States. This continues to be important because most students have no significant exposure to such subject matter in their prior schooling, even in San Francisco.[28]

A strategic example of courses that prepared students for relevant leadership off campus and that provided person power for community

---

28   Malcolm Collier, personal communication with author, May 11, 2018.

organizations was the Coordination of College and Community Resources. This is clearly described by community activist and collaborative leader Gordon Chin:

"I enrolled in an innovative new program developed in 1970 by the Asian American Studies Department and the College of Behavioral and Social Sciences. Officially, it was called Coordination of College and Community Resources, but everyone referred to it as the Nine Unit Block Program. Students enrolled in three BSS courses to support a 20-hour week filed placement in a community organization and were given a small stipend. I chose the Chinatown Youth Center from the 15 Asian American nonprofit options. Although the program only lasted one year due to lack of funding, it was one of the most important and innovative attempts to connect the college to the community.

"Many student participants went on to long-term leadership positions in San Francisco such as Fred Lau (who became Chief of Police), Anita Sanchez (San Francisco Civil Service Director), Jeff Mori (who went on to head the Japanese Community Youth Council), Steve Nakajo (who became Executive Director of Kimochi Kai and Filipino leaders Ed Ilumin and Ed Delacruz (sic) with West Bay Filipino Services."[29]

This example was replicated in other departments to varying degrees.

Being open and inclusive over the years to emerging related areas of scholarship allowed a global outlook and prepared students to be a bridge to the Third World and global views, particularly the migration of human capital in a post-colonial world. For example, the changes in departmental names from Black to Africana studies and from La Raza

---

29   Gordon Chin, *Building Community, Chinatown Style: A Half Century of Leadership in San Francisco Chinatown* (San Francisco: Friends of Chinatown Community Development Center, 2015), 26.

to Latino/Latina studies are comparable to changing racial and ethnic categories in the federal censuses and surveys and reflects the ways that language changes over time. The addition of Race and Resistance Studies in 2010 as a new comparative and interdisciplinary program facilitates introducing relevant new initiatives such as Arab and Muslim Ethnicities and Diasporas.

Through the decades, COES has been able to grant undergraduate and graduate degrees. As of 2018, Bachelor Degrees are offered in Africana Studies, American Indian Education Studies, Asian American Studies, and Latino/Latina Studies. Students can minor in all of these as well as in Race and Resistance Studies. Master's Degrees are offered in Asian American Studies and Ethnic Studies. A recent offering is the Dual Degree Program in the College of Ethnic Studies which was advertised as, "Earn two degrees for the price of one! Students can earn a major and/or a minor in the College of Ethnic Studies in conjunction with another major all within 120 units. Take your general education in Africana Studies, American Indian Studies, Asian American Studies, Latina/Latino Studies, or Race and Resistance Studies and you may be just a few courses away from a degree in the College of Ethnic Studies. American Indian Studies double majors in Anthropology, Biochemistry, Chemistry, History and Music; Asian American Studies double major with Liberal Studies; Latino/Latina Studies double majors with Criminal Justice, Liberal Studies and any other second major; Race and Resistant Studies minor with an outside major in Sociology."[30] This innovation is particularly useful for careers nationally and globally, where cultural competency and multilingual skills are prized. It is another strong example of the interdisciplinary approach that COES holds at its core.

Modeling leadership as a group practice rather than a practice driven by individual egos was key for the BSU/TWLF-led strike to succeed. This filtered down to the individual student organizations and studies. Under the guidance of George Woo and Jim Hirabayashi, the Intercollegiate Chinese Students Association (ICSA), the Asian American Political Alliance (AAPA) and the Philippine American Collegiate Endeavor

---

30 "Dual Degrees with the College of Ethnic Studies," *SFSU*, https://ethnicstudies.sfsu.edu/content/dual-degrees-double-major.

(PACE) used the consensus model in developing the curriculum and administrative procedures for Asian American Studies. In meetings with their respective communities, the student organizations honored their elders by providing them specific time to comment on curriculum and related matters and staying engaged with ongoing communication throughout the planning process. This was also the modus operandi off campus. For example, BSU leaders Arnold Townsend and Benny Stewart, among others, led the fight in concert with strong community leaders, notably Hannibal Williams and Mary Rogers, against redevelopment in the Fillmore via the Western Addition Community Organization (WACO) in the 1960s.[31] From SF State, they went on to other positions. Benny headed up the Marin City Community Development Program. Arnold became a minister of the Without Walls Church.[32]

Continuity and Change across Human Relationships

Material Remembrances, Academic Institutional Contributions and Academic Innovations are concrete examples, among others, of the legacy of SF State COES over 50 years. What has been the most meaningful throughout my life and for the lives of a sizable number of fellow strikers and supporters of SF State College of Ethnic Studies since 1968 is Continuity and Change across Human Relationships.

The Golden Children of 1968 and 1969 at SF State were moved by the real concerns of everyday people, especially our parents and siblings living in segregated neighborhoods and working in dead-end jobs to support their families in the US and in the Third World. We came of age in an era where we honored our parents' and grandparents' sacrifices so that we could go to school, and perhaps even college. We were the generation with access to the American Dream, but barely. We worried about our younger siblings and other children, especially young men of color growing up in Central City, Chinatown, the Bayview, the Mission, the Fillmore and Hunter's Point. During social events of 2018, whether it be the February 11 appreciation for Kenneth Monteiro's twelve years

---

31 "The Fillmore: Mary Rogers," *KQED*, http://www.pbs.org/kqed/ fillmore/learning/people/rogers.html.
32 "Building Communities," *Chinatown Style*, 24.

of service and leadership as the dean of the College of Ethnic Studies or the April 26 screening of *Agents of Change* at UC Berkeley, or the April 27 business meeting of the California State University System-wide Ethnic Studies Council, we see that the relationships across generations and between sisters and brothers of the 1968 and 2016 movements and beyond remain steadfast and highly valued. As noted in chapter 3 "We are Family" and "We Shall Overcome."

For people of color, the ascribed roles of parent, child, and member of both nuclear and extended family are the primary relationships in a person's life. These relationships are multigenerational and include immediate family members, grandparents, and the extended family. In some instances, especially among immigrant communities, familial honorifics such as "Uncle" and "Auntie" are extended to persons from the same neighborhood, village or province. Among those of religious backgrounds, members greet one another and others using terms like "father," "mother," "sister," and "brother." In such ascribed relationships, group solidarity and human connection take precedence. They are terms of affection, not abstract concepts. Thinking globally and acting globally was and continues to be true for diaspora communities. The affirmation of intergenerational bonds signifies that advocating for education for all our children is not limited to time and place but endures across all communities. Such a focus allows for what UC Berkeley ethnic studies and history professor Ronald Takaki called communities of memory. Such a focus allows for days of remembrance as well as speaking to the future.

"Manong" is the Ilocano word for big brother. In ethnic studies, the Ilocano and other Filipino workers who began the 1965 Farmworkers Delano Grape Strike are introduced as such.[33] Historically, the Manongs were internationalists; they had a worldview that understood the breakup of the Spanish colonial empire in the 19th century as the beginning of the social movements in the Third World. They were mentored by the

---

33   Lisa Morehouse, "Grapes of Wrath: the Forgotten Filipinos Who Lead a Farmworker Revolution," *NPR*, https://www.npr.org/sections/thesalt/2015/09/16/440861458/grapes-of-wrath-the-forgotten-filipinos-who-led-a-farmworker-revolution.

Filipino generation before them who led the revolutions against Spain and the United States. After decades of resistance with thousands of supporters, the Manongs were finally evicted from the International Hotel in 1977, as eloquently documented by SF State striker Curtis Choy in *The Fall of the I-Hotel*. Interestingly, in the Seattle area, which also had neighborhoods of people of color, the international theme was also very evident. The neighborhoods of people of color were called the ID, the International District. Since the 1960s, community efforts to resist redevelopment and provide neighborhood services were led by a man that people knew as "Uncle Bob." While SF State had the BSU/TWLF 1968–69, Seattle had the Gang of Four—Roberto Maestas, Bernie Whitebear, Bob Santos and Larry Gossett.[34] Uncle Bob Santos, along with Uncle Fred Cordova of the Filipino American National Historical Society, treated all the young folks, the young bloods, the Young Turks—black, brown, yellow, red and white—as nieces and nephews. More importantly, they envisioned them as current and future local, national, and international leaders and groomed them with tough love. In short, they told us the world was our oyster. The Gang of Four themselves came from interracial and multicultural families.

Many students, faculty, alumni and supporters say the greatest legacy of ethnic studies may be that it feels like family and community. It is like coming home to a place where you are always welcomed as a relative. It is a safe refuge from the demands of a large campus, academic institutions, and the fast-paced, highly technical and highly individualistic mainstream. COES is the heart, where people of color are affirmed by people who look like them; who have similar life experiences, challenges and opportunities; who share their meals, humor, and wisdom. In SF COES, they have role models in people who, in unity, have achieved and continue to achieve against the odds.

---

34   Bob Santos and Gray Iwamoto, *Gang of Four: Four Leaders. Four Communities. One Friendship*, (Seattle: Chin Music Press, 2015).

9 780996 351782